P9-CMZ-544

REVOLUTIONS
IN
MODERN EUROPEAN HISTORY

MAIN THEMES IN EUROPEAN HISTORY

Bruce Mazlish, General Editor

REVOLUTIONS
IN
MODERN EUROPEAN
HISTORY

Edited by

HEINZ LUBASZ
Brandeis University

THE MACMILLAN COMPANY, NEW YORK
COLLIER-MACMILLAN LIMITED, LONDON

FOR HERBERT MARCUSE

First Printing

Library of Congress catalog card number: 66-20213

THE MACMILLAN COMPANY, NEW YORK
COLLIER-MACMILLAN CANADA, LTD., TORONTO, ONTARIO

PRINTED IN THE UNITED STATES OF AMERICA

FOREWORD

History, we are frequently told, is a seamless web. However, by isolating and studying the strands that compose the tapestry of man's past, we are able to discern the pattern, or patterns, of which it is comprised. Such an effort does not preclude a grasp of the warp and woof, and the interplay of the strands; rather, it eventually demands and facilitates such a comprehension. It is with this in mind that the individual volumes of the MAIN THEMES series have been conceived.

The student will discover, for example, that the population changes discussed in one volume relate to the changes in technology traced in another volume; that both changes are affected by, and affect in turn, religious and intellectual developments; and that all of these changes and many more ramify into a complicated historical network through all the volumes. In following through this complex interrelationship of the parts, the student re-creates for himself the unity of history.

Each volume achieves its purpose, and its appeal to a general audience, by presenting the best articles by experts in the field of history and allied disciplines. In a number of cases, the articles have been translated into English for the first time. The individual volume editor has linked these contributions into an integrated account of his theme, and supplied a selected bibliography by means of footnotes for the student who wishes to pursue the topic further. The introduction is an original treatment of the problems in the particular field. It provides continuity and background for the articles, points out gaps in the existing literature, offers new interpretations, and suggests further research.

The volumes in this series afford the student of history an unusual opportunity to explore subjects either not treated, or touched upon lightly in a survey text. Some examples are population—the dramatis personae of history; war—the way of waging peace by other means; the rise of technology and science in relation to society; the role of religious and cultural ideas and institutions; the continuous ebb and flow of exploration and colonialism; and the political and economic works contrived by modern man. Holding fast to these Ariadne threads, the student penetrates the fascinating labyrinth of history.

BRUCE MAZLISH
General Editor

CONTENTS

INTRODUCTION

Revolution is an essentially political process of combat and change. The characteristic weapons of revolutionary combat are political weapons; the characteristic instruments of revolutionary change are political instruments. Yet neither the aims of the revolutionaries nor the actual results of the process of revolution are exclusively or narrowly political. The very essence of revolution is the attempt to alter the conditions of social existence, to lay the foundations for an alternative order of society. Hence revolution is never merely the replacing of one ruling group with another; [1] nor is it a change in the system of government alone. It is generally "a sweeping, fundamental change in political organization, social structure, economic property control and the predominant myth of a social order, thus indicating a major break in the continuity of development." [2]

That the revolutionary process is fundamentally political in nature is underscored by the fact that its beginning and its end are themselves characteristically political: revolution begins with a political crisis and ends with a political settlement.

Revolution begins with a crisis in the state and the launching of an overt attack on the regime. It may be touched off by widespread strikes, mass demonstrations, riots, or armed insurrection. But it is only when and insofar as such activities seek to bring about fundamental innovation and so become part and parcel of a political assault that they constitute revolutionary activity and may precipitate revolution properly so called. It is this clearly political character that distinguishes, for example, the English Revolution of 1640–1660 from a mere civil war and the American Revolution from a mere rebellion. To say that revolution begins with a political crisis is not to deny that revolution is the product of profound, long-range, and widespread changes of many kinds—changes in social

[1] In Professor Brinton's view, revolution does consist essentially in the "drastic, sudden substitution of one group in charge of running a territorial political entity for another group" by means of violence "or some . . . kind of skullduggery." Crane Brinton, *The Anatomy of Revolution*, revised edition (New York: 1952), p. 2.

[2] Sigmund Neumann, "The International Civil War," *World Politics*, 1 (1948–49), pp. 333–350, at p. 333, n. 1.

relations, in economic conditions, in ideas and attitudes, in a country's external relations. But even very dramatic and disruptive changes in economy and society, in thought and in foreign relations, may go on for a long time—perhaps indefinitely—without culminating in revolution. If they do engender revolution, they generally do so by precipitating a grave crisis in the body politic. The long- and short-range causes of this crisis may vary greatly from case to case; but the central issue is always who is to govern and how. Whether we regard revolutions as ultimately the results of class struggles, of shifts in economic relations and circumstances, of subversive ideas, conspiracies, or disappointed expectations, the fact remains that the actual outbreak of revolution is at heart a political event.

By the same token, to say that the process of revolution ends with a political *settlement* is not to deny that revolution has lasting *consequences,* or to maintain that, once the settlement has been achieved, the work of the revolution is over and change and conflict cease. Revolution generates forces and institutions—economic and social, cultural and political, military and diplomatic—which continue to be operative long after the period of overt and intensive upheaval has come to a close. But it is important to note the break between the period of upheaval and the subsequent period of more or less stable and uninterrupted development, between revolutionary upheaval and continuous transformation, between the revolution and the regime that issues from it. This break constitutes what we are calling the "revolution settlement": the point at which the old regime is restored (as it was in England in 1660, in France in 1815) or the new regime emerges safely established and triumphant (as it did in England in 1689, in Russia in 1921). Revolution ends with the victory or defeat of the revolutionary movement but, either way, it ends; and it ends, as it began, with an essentially political event.

The actual course of the revolution is a protracted struggle in which the principal weapons employed by the insurgents are weapons borrowed from the arsenal of state power: political weapons. It is of course true that armed force often plays a significant and at times a decisive role. But it is worth bearing in mind that, in a broad sense, the use of military power in revolution is itself an intrinsically political use. When the modern state, which claims a monopoly of organized military might, turns its armies against an insurgent population, and when the insurgents themselves direct such arms as they can command against their government, armed force becomes simply one of the instruments of political purpose. The fact is that military power is only one aspect—and, in modern European history at any rate, not even the preponderant aspect—of the revolutionary process.[3] In every revolution in modern European history the initial assault, the basis of revolutionary organization, and the characteristic means of combat have been pre-eminently political, in the strict sense of the word.

We may, somewhat schematically, distinguish three phases of revolutionary struggle which frequently merge into one another: the initial assault on the government; the rule of the revolutionary regime; and the defense—successful or not—of the revolutionary regime against counterrevolutionary forces, domestic and foreign.

The first phase is generally a period of increasingly sharp and widespread opposition to the existing system, which culminates in an overt political attack on the government. It sees the emergence of the three indispensable ingredients of a revolutionary movement: leadership, organization, and a program. The insurgents cannot effectively oppose the organized power of the state—government, police, army, and so on—unless they are themselves organized, possess some determined and effectual leaders, and have a more or less comprehensive and coherent program capable of attracting broad support to their cause. This is not to say that the insurgents organize themselves on the spur of the moment or for the express purpose of making a revolution. On the contrary, it has generally been a body already organized for political purposes that has become an insurgent group and has, at least initially, provided the basic leadership and the organizational focus for opposition to the regime. The English Revolutions of 1640 and 1688 were both precipitated by parliamentary groups. The French Revolution of the eighteenth century was unwittingly launched by nobles who in their *parlements* demanded the convoking of yet another political forum, the Estates General. The Russian Revolution began more nearly as a spontaneous popular outburst; but here too the role of organized bodies—the Duma, the workers' soviets, and the clandestine socialist groups—was of decisive practical importance.

When extensive popular opposition coincides with a severe crisis in the body politic, the result is apt to be rebellion. If an organized and well-led group, with a coherent and popular program of systematic change is also present and actively insurgent, the result is likely to be revolution.

The distinction between revolution and rebellion is an important one.

[3] Considerable attention is given to the role of the military element by Chalmers A. Johnson, *Revolution and the Social System* (Stanford: 1964).

The two processes are not unrelated, but they differ in crucial respects. Rebellion, whether by well-formed bands or unorganized masses, is overt opposition directed at particular laws, practices, or individuals. It aims at specific and limited changes. Rebels seek to put an end to intolerable conditions by replacing the personnel of government rather than by transforming the system of domination. They demand the redress of specific grievances rather than a systematic alteration in the foundations of the whole existing order. Even armed rebellion may involve nothing more systematic and fundamental than attacks on isolated individuals whom the rebels hold responsible for their ills—landlords, employers, tax-collectors, hoarders, minor government officials. Rebellion turns into revolution when the demand for particular and limited changes is replaced by a demand for general and fundamental change; when the sovereign power itself is held responsible for prevailing conditions; and when scattered rebellious elements join to form a more or less united revolutionary force. The coming of the French Revolution clearly shows all these processes at work. The separate revolts of nobility, middle classes, urban masses, and peasantry, came together to become a revolutionary movement; the government of Louis XVI was gradually made the chief object of criticism; and the disparate demands for specific reforms gave way to a demand for fundamental changes in the body politic—for a social order based on liberty and equality, for security of person and property, for constitutional government. The gradual emergence of an attack on the government, aimed at changing the constitution and thereby altering the very foundation of a whole range of objectionable conditions, turned mere rebellion into full-fledged revolution. A well-known exchange between the king and one of his courtiers suggests that at least one of them understood the difference. When the fall of the Bastille was reported to the royal court at Versailles, Louis asked the Duke de la Rochefoucauld-Liancourt: "Is this a rebellion?" "No, Sire," replied the duke, "it is a revolution."

If the initial assault on the old regime is successful, it is followed by the rule of a more or less revolutionary government. To what extent and in what directions the new government employs the instruments of combat and change now at its disposal depends on a great number of factors—on its program and its personnel, on the degree of opposition it continues to encounter, on the activities of other groups advocating other changes, and so on. In this brief outline of the nature of revolution we cannot undertake an analysis of these variables or examine the wide variety of ways in which the tools of revolution are wielded. We can simply note that the characteristic weapons which the revolutionary regime employs are precisely the weapons to which the state itself claims an exclusive right: legislation, decree, and executive order; police control, imprisonment, trial, execution, and even terror; confiscation, proscription, and exile—the list might be considerably expanded. The revolutionary regime may be thought of as a counter-government that typically employs all the instruments that are normally at the disposal of the state.

One of these instruments is dictatorship. Lest it be supposed that dictatorship is a form of rule peculiar to revolution, or to "totalitarianism," let us note that dictatorship is a very ancient political institution, devised by the Roman Republic for dealing with emergency situations, and thus originally intended to be a temporary expedient. Revolutionary dictatorship, like the "constitutional dictatorship" instituted by twentieth-century democracies in time of war, is usually conceived of by its instigators as a temporary device, as an emergency measure to tide the country over its crisis and to undertake all the most urgent steps of direction, mobilization, combat, and reform. The most famous of these revolutionary dictatorships are those of Cromwell, Robespierre, and Lenin. The first of these died of inanition; the second was overthrown by force; the third survived. Having survived three years of war and counterrevolution, Lenin's dictatorship was transformed into a permanent instrument of government which could be very dictatorial indeed without necessarily being revolutionary. As dictatorship became a permanent fixture in Russia, less and less was heard about its being a temporary expedient, though the fiction was maintained that the dictatorship was not one of government over the governed, but rather one of the victorious proletariat over the defeated counterrevolutionary classes. The Soviet dictatorship is, to be sure, the child of revolution; but that is very far from making it, half a century later, a revolutionary dictatorship.

The defense of the revolutionary regime constitutes the final phase of the revolution, and terminates in the victory or defeat of that regime. It consists in the conflict between the revolutionary forces and their opponents, domestic and foreign. Adherents and allies of the old regime may attempt to oust the revolutionary government, to reinstate those who formerly enjoyed power and privilege, and to restore the old order either *in toto* or in modified form. The struggle itself may be quite mild, as it was in England in the late 1650's. But it may also involve civil and international war at their most ferocious, as it did in France in the mid-1790's and in Russia between 1918 and 1921. Now, once again, as in the first phase, the part played by armed forces may be of great moment. By this time the revolutionary regime generally disposes of a very substantial military force. Even if it does, it can still be defeated "from without" by a combination of domestic counterrevolutionary forces and armed foreign intervention. But it may also fall victim to a *coup d'état* "from within": it may be overthrown by one of the members of the regime itself, or by one of its generals—as witness the counterrevolutionary coups of the two Napoleons. Last but not least the revolution may simply collapse from lack of impetus and popular support and end in a peaceable restoration, like that of Charles II of England in 1660.

With the end of this third phase, the revolution itself comes to a close, to be followed by a period of comparative stability and domestic peace. The revolution that began when the monopoly of political power in the state was successfully challenged ends when that monopoly is re-established—in old hands or in new.[4] In contrast to the endless processes of social conflict and transformation, revolution as a process is terminable, temporary. What is sometimes called *permanent revolution* is in fact nothing but a process of continuous transformation under the auspices of government, a process from which the overthrow of the existing regime, which is an essential part of revolution properly so called, is conspicuously absent. This is not to deny that the process of transformation from above, of change directly engineered by government, is a very important political phenomenon, significantly different from the process of social change in which the role of government is indirect. But it is desirable, for the sake of clarity, to recognize that direct intervention by government in every aspect of social existence, no matter how dynamic it may be, is not synonymous with revolution.

Does the regime that issues from revolution actually represent the political foundation of that alternative order of society which it was the object of the revolutionary movement to establish? If the revolutionary movement is defeated, the projected alternative (together with its principal protagonists) may at first be completely suppressed in counterrevolution, reaction, and white terror. But to some degree, and in modified form, it often finds its way into the order which the restoration eventually establishes. It would seem that, though revolution may fail to triumph, once it has won at least a temporary success, its work cannot

[4] *Cf.* Peter Amann, "Revolution: A Redefinition," *Political Science Quarterly*, 77 (1962), pp. 36–53, at p. 39: "As I define it, revolution prevails when the state's monopoly power is effectively challenged and persists until a monopoly of power is re-established."

be wholly undone. Its partisans may not remain in power; but they continue to press, by other means or even in subsequent revolutions, for the changes they deem indispensable. What if the revolutionary movement is victorious? In every great revolution involving large masses of people, there is always more than one projected alternative, more than one insurgent group, more than one revolutionary program. In the course of the upheaval one or another of them may be dominant for a time. But the close of the revolution generally means defeat for all but one of these alternatives. From the point of view of the population as a whole, therefore, even the victory of the revolution is never complete, if only because it involves not merely the defeat of the old order but also the defeat of every alternative but one. Cromwell's victory, temporary as it proved to be, spelled defeat for the royalists; but it also meant defeat for the radical left wing of the revolutionary movement. Lenin's victory put an end to tsarism; but it also eliminated the democratic alternative.

The regime that issues from revolution is always a less than complete embodiment of the new and better society it was intended to establish. How much of an achievement, how much of an advance a given revolution represents has to be judged, not in absolute terms, but in terms of what was concretely possible, and by comparing the new society with the one that preceded it. For, when all is said and done, revolution itself does not spring from a theoretical interest in a wholly perfect social order so much as from an urgent desire to find some viable alternative to conditions that are felt to be intolerable.

PLEBEIAN UPRISINGS IN FRANCE PRECEDING THE FRONDE (1623–1648) *

B. F. Porshnev †

Historical scholarship divides the whole history of social movements in the towns of the Middle Ages into three stages: (1) the struggle of the town as a whole against its seigneur; (2) the struggle of the burghers (especially the guild-masters) who were excluded from municipal power, against the patricians; and (3) the struggle of the urban plebs against one or another of their exploiters. We know that at various times in history these three forms of class struggle intermingle or are superimposed upon one another in very complex ways. But in the life of the French town of the seventeenth century we find only occasional echoes and survivals of the first two forms. The overwhelming mass of facts has to be related entirely to the third category, that of plebeian movements in the town. In the present case these take the form specifically of a struggle against royal taxation.[1]

* The mid-seventeenth century was a period of revolution and rebellion in many parts of Europe, from Catalonia to the Ukraine, from Holland to Sicily. In France, years of sporadic opposition to government culminated in the great rebellion known as the Fronde, which broke out in 1648. Until recently, historical writing on that rebellion has dealt chiefly with the Fronde of the Princes and that of the Parlements. In 1948 Academician Porshnev (University of Moscow) published a detailed study of the popular opposition, rural and urban, during the twenty-five years preceding the Fronde. The following selection from his book presents his analysis of the basic characteristics of the plebeian opposition in the towns.

† B. F. Porshnev, *Narodnie Vostaniia vo Frantsii pered Frondoi (1623–1648)* [Popular Uprisings in France Preceding the Fronde (1623–1648)] (Moscow: 1948), pp. 280, 282, and 283–299, with minor deletions and omission of footnotes. Translated from the Russian by Melissa Nelken and Heinz Lubasz. Two important reviews of the book by French students of the period have recently been published: Robert Mandrou, "Les soulèvements populaires et la société française au XVIIe siècle," *Annales,* **14** (1959), pp. 756–765; and Roland Mousnier, "Recherches sur les soulèvements populaires en France avant la Fronde," *Revue d'histoire moderne et contemporaine,* **5** (1958), pp. 81–113.

[1] The urban uprisings examined by Professor Porshnev are listed here for the convenience of the student. [Ed.]

1623 in Rouen, Marseilles, Poitiers;

1624 in Niort, Lyons, Figeac, Cahors;

One can, to be sure, point to a certain number of plebeian uprisings not specifically directed against taxes. . . . There are, however, good grounds for thinking that even these uprisings . . . were in fact called forth by the pressure of taxation. The commercial and industrial bourgeoisie usually found some device for shifting taxes affecting their interests onto the shoulders of the popular masses. In such cases it was not the taxes themselves, but these devices, which served as the immediate occasions for popular uprisings. . . .

It is important to note that, though the taxes which served as the immediate occasions for uprisings were various, and though the uprisings themselves sometimes came to an end with the announcement that the tax at issue would be deferred or abolished, nevertheless, in the minds of the people these taxes were not separate and distinct: all "financiers," i.e., all the persons involved with any tax whatever, were called the same names: *maltôtiers* (extortionists) and *gabeleurs;* and violence against them all was usually the slogan of the uprisings.

Thus the uprising of 1628 in Laval was provoked by the creation of

---

1625 in Troyes;
1626 in Auxerre, Amiens, Blaye;
1627 in Troyes, Bergerac, Bordeaux, Villefranche-de-Rouergue;
1628 in Troyes, Amiens, Laval, Rouen, Cognac, Auxerre;
1629 in Lyons, Angoulême, Saint-Jean-d'Angely, Saintes;
1630 in Dijon, Grenoble, Nantes, Poitiers, Orléans, Caen, Lyons, Angers;
1631 in Paris, Bordeaux, Fontenay, Marseilles, Orléans, Aix-en-Provence;
1632 in Toulouse, Lyons, Poitiers;
1633 in Chavigny, Dax, Moulins, Niort, Auvillar (precise date in dispute), Mont-de-Marsan (precise date in dispute);
1634 in Rouen;
1635 in Bordeaux, Agen, Périgueux, Moissac, Lectoure, Castelsarrasin, Auvillar, Montech, Beaumont-de-Lomagne, Auch, La Réole, Condom, Nérac, Astaffort (?), Port-Sainte-Marie, Luzech, Bazas, Monferran, Toulouse, Narbonne;
1636 in Châlons-sur-Marne, Rennes, Amiens, Abbeville;
1637 in Bergerac, Eymet, Périgueux, Saint-Foy-la-Grand, Cahors;
1638 in Grenade, Saintes;
1639 in Rouen, Caen, Avranches, Vire, Bayeux, Coutances, Mortain, Bourg, Poitiers;
1640 in Aurillac, Moulins, Clermont, Poitiers, Galan;
1641 in Bayonne, Angers, Grenoble, Sables-d'Olonne, Limoges;
1642 in Clermont, Lyons;
1643 in Villefranche-de-Rouergue, Najac, Saint-Salvadour, Issoire, Tours, Angers, Angoulême;
1644 in Marseilles, Arles, Romans, Valence, Dax;
1645 in Montpellier, Besiers, Mende, Beauvais;
1647 in Tours.

the offices of overseer and inspector of linen manufacture. "But," in the words of Pagès, "the people, once they had been aroused, set out after all those who in their eyes represented the royal Treasury." The crowd sacked the house of the collector of the taille [a direct tax on income and/or land], pursued the collector of the salt-tax and the guard charged with preventing the smuggling of salt, all the while shouting: "death to the gabeleurs!" As an uprising developed further and became deeper, the circle of people brought under this odious concept generally became wider and wider, until it comprised all the defenders of order, all those who profited by the poverty of the people, and the like. Correspondingly, the word *gabelle* came to have a special significance for the popular masses: it referred not only to the government tax on salt, but also to any illegal and burdensome tax in general, and even to any threat of the imposition of a new tax. Sometimes rumors sufficed to make a crowd rise against an unspecified *gabelle*. Let us recall the previously cited letter of November, 1645 [discussed in an earlier chapter] from the Duke d'Epernon to Mazarin and Séguier, informing them of the establishment of control points in various parts of Languedoc to help the salt-tax collector: "I would point out to you, Monsieur, that the very name 'gabelle' arouses the people of this region to such an extent—even when it does not concern them—that they are beside themselves when they so much as hear talk of it."

This typical feature of the course of the uprisings—that they are initially touched off by some particular innovation in taxes (at times even by a not very substantial one, such as the tax on tavern-keepers which raised a storm in Guyenne in 1635), but then readily broaden their programs and battle fronts—confirms our above-mentioned views, that one should distinguish the occasions for the uprisings from their causes. The multiplicity of occasions only underscores the uniformity of the causes.

Where, then, are the underlying causes of the uprisings to be found? Undoubtedly in the fact that in the French town of the 1620's, 30's, and 40's a large segment of the population lived at such a low level economically that the slightest deterioration in their circumstances immediately threatened their very existence. Abundant evidence to this effect may be found in the Séguier archives: the words *misery, desperation,* occur over and over again in the reports. There is a letter from the intendant Argenson, written at Limoges in March 1633, which makes a profound impression: he writes about the dreadful poverty prevalent in Limoges, about the death by plague of an enormous part of the population of the town, "in which few artisans are left" and even the surviving burghers are in dire straits. He therefore requests that the collection of new taxes in Limoges be deferred. In September 1636 the Duke de Bellegarde, governor of Burgundy, draws a sad picture of conditions in Clamecy, "which is very small" and full of poor people. "Having been forced for so long to spend my time among these poor people," he cannot but feel compassion towards them; and he requests that they be granted remission of the new military tax, which is beyond their means. One could cite numerous similar testimonies.

This poverty itself was the underlying cause of the uprisings. It was not taxation alone which gave birth to this broad layer of impoverished people in the French towns: just as in the countryside taxation merely completed the ruin of a peasantry exploited by feudal lords, so in the towns the development of an indigent stratum resulted from the steady advance of capitalist exploitation. The yoke of taxation merely made the existence of this segment of the urban population forcefully evident. It uncovered what was hidden in the economic depths. It brought the poor to a state of paupery and sharply etched the line which separated them from the well-to-do.

The sources often emphasize that uprisings were carried out by those "who had nothing to lose." This specification lends weight to the identification of the social character of the urban uprisings as plebeian. On the other hand, in the great majority of cases the sources call those responsible for the uprisings either simply "people" (*peuple* or *peuples*) or, more precisely, "common people" (*populace*), "rabble" (*canaille*), "humble people" (*menu peuple*), "lowly people" (*bas peuple*), "scum" (*lie*), "base persons" (*infimes personnes*), "the lowest sector of the populace" (*la plus basse partie du peuple*). All these terms seem to be rather indefinite and to encompass too motley a conglomeration of various urban social elements. But this variety fully corresponds to the heterogeneity and complexity of that natural blending which Marx and Engels termed the "plebeian elements of a town" or, more simply, "the plebeians." For them this category did not express the static relationships of feudal-corporative or of bourgeois society, but rather the dynamics of the transformation of one into the other. The plebeians are not yet even the pre-proletariat: they form an ill-assorted and heterogeneous mass, rooted in various groupings of feudal society; but at the same time they are gradually coalescing into a real whole. Their common characteristic is the lack or the loss of property, and the performance of paid physical labor in the town. As this common trait gradually became more pronounced, it cut into and broke through the lines along which the urban populace of the Middle Ages had earlier been divided.

"The plebeian opposition," says Engels, "consisted of burghers in reduced circumstances and of the mass of urban dwellers who were excluded from the rights of citizenship: the artisans' apprentices, the journeymen workers, and the numerous members of an incipient *lumpenproletariat.*" According to Engels the urban plebs were composed of three elements: (1) the embryonic manufacturing and artisan preproletariat, undifferentiated as yet from the plebeian mass; i.e., the hired workers and especially the apprentices, who "were outside official society and, in terms of their living conditions, were as close to being a proletariat as was possible, given the conditions of industry of that day"; (2) the mass of petty artisans, "impoverished members of the guilds who were connected to the existing civic order through their privileges," but actually were already losing their former economic independence; and (3) "a large number of people of no definite occupation and no fixed place of residence," that is, primarily the *déclassé* elements from the countryside —"evicted peasants and discharged servants" who sought a livelihood in the towns. Among the latter one can distinguish the completely *déclassé* "beggars" and "vagrants" from those who were gradually absorbed into the economic life of the town as casual laborers, unskilled workers, and so on—"seeking their meager subsistence in the town by casual labor and whatever else happened not to require membership in a guild,"—i.e., approaching the condition of an incipient pre-proletariat. Although this analysis by Engels of the plebeians relates to the German town of the sixteenth century, it can on the whole be applied to the French town of the seventeenth century as well. The same three elements can indeed be traced among the participants in urban uprisings; it is just these that contemporary observers group together under the terms "common people," "humble people," and so on.

Apprentices (*garçons, valets, compagnons*) are often identified as the offenders and instigators in uprisings. During the uprising of 1640 in Poitiers, for example, a hatter's apprentice (*garçon chapelier*) who stood at the head of a crowd, was killed; in Bordeaux in 1635, an apprentice (*compagnon*) cooper; in Agen in 1635, a spurmaker's apprentice; and so on. Yet we have no direct indications that associations of apprentices as such played a role in the uprisings. This may be due simply to the clandestine nature of these organizations, since there is often a firm basis for suspecting their participation: for instance, in the weavers' revolt of

1636 in Amiens, in the Dijon uprising of 1630, and others. Information regarding the journeymen's associations in the seventeenth century is meager, though their existence and activity is incontestable, judging, for example, by the 1601 resolution of the Parlement of Paris prohibiting associations and assemblies of shoemakers' apprentices, the resolution of 1631 prohibiting associations of carpenters' apprentices, and so on. In 1639 a denunciation was received at the Sorbonne concerning the existence of "impious, blasphemous, and superstitious" associations of apprentice shoemakers, saddlers, tailors, hatters, and cutlers. The Sorbonne's resolution condemning and prohibiting such organizations was not published until 1655. There we read, *inter alia:* "The alleged duty of the apprentice consists in three vows: to honor God, to preserve his master's possessions, and to support his fellows. But, quite on the contrary, these apprentices greatly dishonor God by profaning all the mysteries of our religion, ruining their masters by emptying their shops of workers as soon as any member of their cabal complains that he has been mistreated, and ruining themselves by the fines which they impose on one another, only to use them for drinking. They have their own court, they elect officers, . . . maintain a network of connections between towns, and have a password . . . form an aggressive alliance against apprentices in their trade who do not belong to their cabal, beating and maltreating them." There is good reason to think that these associations—anti-Church in their organization and anti-State by the fact of their illegality—must have played an important role during the uprisings.

It is quite difficult to distinguish, in the terminology of sources and writers, the apprentices from the "servants" (*serviteurs*) who are mentioned as active participants in the uprisings; it is often clearly implied that these servants are in fact apprentices. An even more general term, again partly comprising apprentices, is *workers* (*ouvriers*).

It is sometimes possible to get some idea of just who these *ouvriers* were by studying the economic character of the town itself. Thus, all the information about the uprising in Lyons in 1632 indicates that such *ouvriers* were its motive force; and we may confidently conclude that they constituted a manufacturing-industrial pre-proletariat, since it is well known that Lyons was comparatively highly developed industrially. It is possible, by analogy with the Lyons uprising, to construct a picture of a number of others in which the principal participants were designated *workers.* Although the sources and the historians occasionally use the term *ouvriers* rather vaguely, most of them deal with industrially more or less developed towns; and this provides some basis for making the same inferences as in the case of Lyons. . . .

A scarcely perceptible line separated these *ouvriers* from the second plebeian element, the petty guild and non-guild artisans who constituted the active leadership in other uprisings. Two contemporary observers could define the very same uprising differently—the one, as the act of "workers," the other as that of artisans of a certain profession. It is in fact impossible to separate the two elements precisely. We have, however, never found the slightest trace of any involvement on the part of the guilds as such in the course of an uprising. This would seem to warrant the conclusion that the higher echelons of the guilds never participated in these movements. What is more, there are cases in which the socio-economic division within a guild made itself apparent in the course of an uprising. The uprising of 1634 in Rouen, which was provoked by a new tax on fells, was led by tanners; not only were the houses of tax agents destroyed, but also those of two or three powerful master-tanners who were representatives of the highest levels of the trade. In other words, the movements clearly did not have a corporate character. . . . A careful examination of the course and nature of these uprisings reveals that they were by no means movements of artisans' guilds, such as had frequently occurred in French towns in previous centuries, but were, rather, plebeian movements of a new type, supported, not by a particular professional corporation, a guild, but by a particular social stratum in the population.

The role of leading or instigating an uprising, which fell now to this profession, now to that, is to be explained largely in terms of the concrete occasion leading to each individual outburst. The spark came from the group directly burdened by a new tax, and quickly spread to the others. Such diffusion may be observed in almost every instance, provided the movement did not die out or get suppressed at its inception. The slogan "down with the gabeleurs, the monopolists, the partisans" [*"sus aux gabeleurs, aux accapareurs, aux partisans"*] was equally comprehensible to all levels of the urban plebs and easily united them against a common enemy. Floquet has shown very convincingly in the case of Rouen how the narrowly professional disputes which divided various groups of workers and artisans gradually disappeared in the series of popular "revolts": "now," he notes, "having established an entente, they always march forth united."

It would, therefore, be quite incorrect to draw conclusions from the profession of individual participants or leaders sometimes mentioned in the sources, as to the professional or social basis of a given uprising. For instance, from the fact that a hatmaker's apprentice led the rebellious crowd of Poitiers in 1640 or that a tailor distinguished himself in one of the skirmishes by giving the mayor of the town a beating, no direct inferences may be made as to the professional composition of this crowd. The frequent presence of representatives of several professions at the head of a single uprising ought to serve as an additional warning against identifying the profession of the leaders with the professional composition of the whole uprising. . . .

It would be far more interesting to have a complete inventory of all the professions whose representatives are mentioned in the sources as leaders or active participants in the uprisings. But the meagerness and the haphazard nature of our information make it impossible even to contemplate any sort of complete picture and, consequently, to draw any general conclusions. Here is a list, solely for purposes of illustration, of different artisans (and petty tradesmen) who are mentioned in the cited materials. We list first those that are mentioned several times or in the plural, and at the end those mentioned only singly: shoemaker, bootmaker, boatman, cooper, tanner, dyer, locksmith, mason, porter, draper, wool carder, weaver (specifically: silk weaver, velvet weaver, cotton weaver, serge weaver), paper maker, cardboard maker, joiner, blacksmith, tailor, drayman, tavern-keeper, butcher, fishmonger (male and female), skin-dresser, saddler, glover, currier, hatter, carpenter, glazier, furrier, watchmaker, gunsmith (side-arms maker), pastry-cook, cook, inn-keeper. The great majority of these people belong to the poorest artisan professions, often ones not organized into guilds and therefore most ruinously affected by the advance of capitalism. Many of them undoubtedly were apprentices and workers. Of those at the end of the above list, who were mentioned only once, some belong to the more prosperous professions; however, we may assume that they were either apprentices or such artisans as were unable to remain at the level of the rich masters of their profession, were obliged to work for them, and merged into the mass of the urban plebs.

There is, finally, the third element of the plebs—consisting of the *déclassé* peasantry, the *lumpenproletariat*—which is also strongly represented among the participants in the urban uprisings. It was just this element which made up the substance of the suburban population which was so often significantly involved in the uprisings. In keeping with the dual nature of this element, referred to above, we find, on the one hand, numerous references to the participation of "beggars," "vagrants," "men without kin" (*"les gens sans aveu"*), "men without hearth or home"; Boissonnade, for example, describes the start of the 1639 uprising in Poitiers as follows: "On August first, in the slums of Chaussée and Saint-Sulpicien, the meeting-grounds of vagabonds and 'caymans' [*caimans*: literally, "alligators"], where the miserable multitude teemed, ready for any excess, men and women formed themselves into armed bands." On the other hand, day-laborers, loaders, porters, barrowers, street peddlers, and boatmen (these last can also be partly considered as artisans) are often met with among the active participants in uprisings. These were people who, though *déclassé,* gradually integrated themselves into the economy of the town and earned their living there—though, like the Dijon day-laborers mentioned above, they sometimes still kept one foot in the countryside.

An action characteristic of this stratum of society was the uprising in Rouen in 1623. It was provoked by an attempt on the part of the crown to exact fees for such "offices" as ragman, barrower, loader and packer of cargo, wood peddler, collier, street vendor of onions, apples, oranges, oysters; and, according to Floquet, "hundreds of other petty occupations of this kind." In Normandy there were about 10,000 such "officials"; in Rouen alone, where the uprising occurred, there were 4,000. A few months after the uprising the Estates of Normandy wrote with displeasure in their cahier about the tax-farmers who had provoked the uprising, that they "had sought to exact tribute from the suffering, the sweat, and the arduous toil of the common people, by raising to the level of official positions the most despised and base" occupations, which provided "so little income and wages for these lowly people and . . . for the hired hands like them, who endured heat and cold, that many of them could not earn even two or three sous a day for their sustenance." The element of the urban population so strikingly described here appears to have participated, to a varying extent, in all the urban uprisings.

We have every reason, then, to identify the plebs as the fundamental moving force of the urban uprisings studied, and to call these uprisings plebeian uprisings. It is important to note that it was precisely the most *déclassé* stratum of the plebs which served as a sort of direct connecting link between these uprisings and those of the peasants: as we have seen in the case of Dijon, Bordeaux, and so on [discussed in an earlier chapter], the suburbs formed the link between the towns and the countryside.

The extraordinarily important role played by women in the uprisings, not only as participants but also as leaders and agitators inciting to rebellion, must be mentioned in the context of this inquiry into the composition of the insurgents. Many of the episodes related by the sources are connected with the activities of women. Women's names are frequently recorded in such lists of executed leaders as have come down to us. Sometimes women constitute the basic mass of the rebels, in which case the sources speak of the whole uprising as a "women's rebellion." Thus, in Grenoble in 1641, an uprising against a new tax on salt was secretly engineered by women who, armed with halberds and sticks, even set upon the tax agents and, simultaneously, the consuls of the town. They succeeded in getting the newly-imposed tax abolished. A very typical example of a "women's rebellion" was examined above [in an earlier chapter]: the one in Valence in 1644, when the intendant Fouquet and two councillors of the Parlement of Grenoble had to defend themselves against a crowd of armed women.

Finally, let us note the not insignificant role of youth in the uprisings, to judge by the frequent references to "urchins" [*gamins*] and by the references to some of the offenders in the lists of those condemned, or excluded from an amnesty, simply as "son of so-and-so." It is quite possible that most of these were artisans' apprentices.

The tactics of the plebeian uprisings varied considerably. Sometimes the signal for the start of an uprising was given by a tocsin rung from one or another of the bell-towers of the town. Usually it all began with spontaneous acts of violence against the fiscal agents, especially the hated *gabeleurs*. Then began the destruction of the tax offices, in the course of which papers, tax lists, and even movable property were also destroyed. The private houses of finance, municipal, and judicial officials were also sacked, and sometimes those of other prosperous burghers as well. The official sources usually note the absence of thievery and plundering, while the private sources, such as the chronicle of Malebesse in Agen and others, are inclined to make much of instances in which private property was seized and plunder was threatened. The crowds were armed with halberds, iron objects, stones, sticks, and whatever else was handy; more rarely they had swords, lances, and broadswords; more rarely still, firearms. Usually they moved in a mass or in several bands from one object of destruction to another. Where the uprising for a time gained the upper hand, they seized the town hall and the adjacent prison, and freed the inmates. When they could, they seized even the town fortifications and the fortress wall, and opened the gates to the inhabitants of the suburbs and the surrounding villages. The struggle for the town gates was often the center of attention, both for the authorities and for the insurgents: on its outcome depended the possibility of merging the plebeian uprising with a peasant one. The street skirmishes and battles were carried on hand-to-hand; sometimes cobblestones, pulled out of the pavement, rained down on the attacking troops. In many cases the insurgents very effectively employed the threat of setting the whole town on fire—an awful threat in the almost wholly wooden French towns of the seventeenth century. In the course of the struggles both the authorities and the insurgents at times erected barricades. The methods of combat could vary greatly, depending on local conditions and on the course of the uprising itself. In Bayonne for example, in 1641, the insurgents, having seized the town artillery, fitted out a small rebel flotilla against the royal ship.

In the course of an uprising, leaders would invariably arise who directed the actions of the crowds; they were the agitators who aroused them. Sometimes, though rarely, the leaders were not plebs in the strict sense but rather the lower strata of the town "intelligentsia": minor employees of the judiciary (drawn from among those who did not enjoy the rights and privileges accorded to bourgeois officials); still more rarely, a representative of the lower clergy; and once, a doctor. Generally the leaders came from the plebeian mass. In several cases—as, for example, in Bayonne in 1641—mention is made of attempts by the authorities to bribe these plebeian leaders; but it appears that these attempts were only very rarely successful (as they were, for example, in Bordeaux in 1635). Upon the suppression of an uprising those leaders who had not perished in the streets either succeeded in escaping, or were subjected to repressive measures, which at best meant permanent exile from the town and the province.

It is impossible, however, to speak of any actual organization or formal discipline among the insurgent crowds: the uprisings had a spontaneous character. Only rarely do we detect signs of a measure of organization among the insurgents and find something like a general staff. . . . Moreover, it is sometimes possible, despite the inadequacies of our sources, to observe definite advance preparations for an uprising. . . . Uprisings in different towns usually flared up separately. A direct link among them is only rarely to be observed, if we discount the inflammatory rumors about events in other towns and the rather unclear role of those who figure in the sources as "strangers," "vagrants," "people without hearth or home" [*"les gens sans toit ni foyer"*], who sometimes appeared in the towns before the start of an uprising, perhaps carrying the contagion of rebellion. The appearance of such "professional agitators" may have been furthered by the judicial practice of exiling active participants following an uprising, and by the fact that many of them had probably fled their homes under the threat of repressions. However, the cases we have instanced of definite advance preparations are so many instances of closer ties with simultaneous uprisings in other towns, both near by and at some distance. The uprising in Niort in 1633 apparently occurred as a result of direct relations with the then insurgent towns in the regions of Poitou and Guyenne; the uprisings in Bordeaux, Périgueux, and Agen in 1635 belong, as we saw, to a group of interconnected uprisings in southwestern France; the uprising in Poitiers in 1639 was connected with that of the *nu-pieds* in Normandy.

The tendency of the uprisings to become widely diffused can be very clearly observed in many cases. On the one hand, the insurgent plebs of one town would endeavor to arouse the inhabitants of neighboring towns. This was necessary not only in order to increase the force of the uprising as a whole, but also in order to minimize the negative effect which the example of obedient neighbors might have on the undecided elements in the insurgent town. Emissaries and sometimes even written appeals were sent out, calling for support and union with the uprising. On the other hand, the neighbors themselves were easily attracted by the example of a successful uprising. At times even the false rumor of an uprising in another town was enough of a stimulus to precipitate a plebeian rising. The example of those who agreed to pay a tax had a dampening effect, while that of those who refused inspired others to opposition. The governor of Limousin, the Duke de Ventadour, writes to the Chancellor in July 1637 about the attempts to collect a compulsory loan or "offering" [*offrande*] from the towns. The inhabitants of Limoges refused to make this "offering"; and "the other towns of the province await their example," since "the majority think that their poverty exempts them from such an offering." But if Limoges serves as an example to the other towns of Limousin, it is itself recalcitrant because it follows the example of towns in other provinces: "the consuls have assured me that it is impossible for them to propose to the inhabitants that they give a larger amount of money, without running the risk of great injury to themselves," since "the people know that not a single town in the surrounding provinces has agreed to offer the said loans." Altogether, the term "bad example" is encountered frequently in the reports of intendants and officials on the uprisings in the towns. Consequently the lateral diffusion of uprisings was, to the minds of contemporaries, a usual phenomenon. Similarly, severe punishment of an insurgent town was discussed in administrative correspondence as an "example" and a "lesson" for other towns—striking indirect evidence that the plebeian movements were by no means as isolated from one another or as heterogeneous as might appear at first glance. The plebs' horizon was far from being limited by the boundaries of their own towns. The excessive localization of the uprisings by French local historians reflects their conceptions rather than historical reality.

The repercussions of every plebeian uprising spread not only in space but also in time. It is unnecessary to repeat here the findings we reported in the preceding chapter: the effects of every uprising last for many years; not one of them fails to leave its mark on the consciousness and the subsequent conduct of the plebeian mass. "The slaughter is still too recent"; "the uprising is still too vividly remembered"—such warnings are sometimes issued by intendants when the government proposes to introduce a new tax. We saw, in the case of Aix, the direct line of succession linking the uprising of 1631 with the events of 1643 and, even beyond that, with those of the Fronde. Similar linkages were observed in other cases. Here a very general statement will suffice: the Fronde came as if on the crest of an enormous wave made up of the numerous separate plebeian uprisings—uniting them in itself as a result of their capacity to engender repercussions in space and time. All the plebeian uprisings of a quarter-century united as though in a single focus, in the nationwide political crisis known as the Fronde.

The ideology of the plebeian uprisings was not distinguished either by profundity or by clarity. The demands of the insurgents expressed only their immediate goal: abolition of the latest tax. But, as we have said, every specific tax was easily subsumed under the general concept of fiscal extortion, *maltôte, gabelle.* The usual slogans of the uprisings were the cries "death to the *gabeleurs!*" "let's have at the *gabeleurs* . . . the extortionists . . . the monopolists!" and the like. Was this program of opposition to taxes linked with wider socio-political perspectives? In his memoirs Richelieu writes as follows about the uprisings of 1635: "The rebels were aroused not only by the war into which they saw the King plunged on all sides, but also by the false reports being spread that the King's affairs were going badly while his enemies prospered." He adds that the rebels were in the end encouraged by an accident that befell the king, which they took as a bad omen for him. As he was returning from the hunt near Monceaux, lightning struck so close to his carriage that the coachman was actually burned: "these wicked Frenchmen interpreted this episode as a warning to the King from on high." We must not, however, give too radical a sense to Richelieu's testimony. The political thinking of the plebeian masses remained basically monarchist; the political ideology of the uprisings for the most part did not go beyond such slogans as "Long live the king—without taxes!" "Long live the king—without the *gabelle!*" and the like. But let us not forget that these very slogans were the slogans of the Fronde and, one hundred and fifty years later, of the Revolution of 1789. Let us also not exaggerate the significance of the traditional toasts to the king's health: abstracted from taxation and from all those authorities—called *gabeleurs* by the people—which in practice defended the tax system, the king virtually became an almost empty fiction. In the above-mentioned reports from the Séguier archives we found several testimonies and anxious accounts of the declining authority of the royal power in the minds of the people. Here, for instance, is one intendant's advice: "since we do not live in a time when it is necessary thoughtlessly to mistreat the people . . . useless severity only tears from their hearts such devotion to the ruler as they still have." In his *Political Testament* Richelieu himself states that increases in taxation lead to the disappearance of "love and fidelity" to the king and bring the people's curses on him, endangering "the existence of the State and the safety of the King's person." It is possible, albeit rarely, to observe movements against the very person of the king in some of the uprisings, as for example in Amiens in 1628. The note sent to Richelieu by the Superintendant of Finance, Bullion—along with a report on the uprising drawn up by some long-suffering official (a *maître de requêtes*)—is characteristic: "This is a serious matter. . . . It sets a most dangerous example when, in a town which has a citadel, the governor is unable to put down an uprising, and an emissary of the King's of so high a rank as *maître de requêtes* is forced to flee the town, to the accompaniment of abuse against the sacred person of our King." The arrival of the emissary, who had come on administrative and fiscal business, was accompanied by a rumor to the effect that he was also to "impose taxes on all goods." During the night, the house in which he was staying was surrounded by an armed crowd of ten thousand which blocked all the adjacent streets and alleys. The intendant managed to get to the town hall, where he was given a horse on which to flee under the protection of a dozen local nobles. In his report he writes that the armed battalions of the town militia, "instead of suppressing the uprising, tried several times to attack and kill us with their muskets and lances, . . . having been incited thereto by the more than ten thousand people who pursued us with horrible insults, even against the person of the King." This is not a unique instance. In the Dijon uprising of 1630 a portrait of Louis XIII was burned; not only were portraits of Richelieu and the Superintendant of Finance, d'Effiat, burned in a bonfire during the uprising in Aix in 1631, but insults were hurled at the king's portrait which, according to one witness, "they were ready to tear down," and, according to another, they dragged through the mud and cut up with knives. The crowd also threatened to beat up the priests who were praying for the king.

The sources repeatedly attest to manifestations of hatred against Richelieu and Mazarin, whom the people considered the principal authors of their misfortunes. But was there any clear socio-political ideal behind such confused discontent with the existing regime? Clearly not. The plebeian mass could be swayed by the most reactionary slogans, such as the separatist cry, "Long live the Emperor!" which may have figured in the 1630 uprising in Dijon. We do not find, however, either slogans or demands concerned with the restoration of any of the civic or corporate privileges of medieval times. Quite unclear is the political content of the slogan in the name of which the anti-fiscal plebeian uprising at Poitiers developed in 1640: "Long live the king and the people's freedom!" (*"Vive le roi et la franchise publique"*).

Finally, in the Niort uprising of 1624, we encounter an ideological motif common in the peasant and plebeian movements of the Middle Ages: the negation of private property. This case can all the more be considered an echo of the sectarian "communism" of the Middle Ages as it, likewise, was led by a monk, Calixte, "who, in the markets of the town, preached insurrection and declared the pillaging of stores of food to be legitimate."

To the student interested in penetrating the psychology of mass behavior during both the plebeian and the peasant uprisings before the Fronde, the positive elements—the slogans, the programs, the goals—are not as important as the negative ones: the weakening, carefully and frequently documented, of the ideological reins keeping the masses in obedience to the existing regime. The people do not heed persuasion, they have become *"déraisonnable"*; arguments and reasons have no effect on them—that is uniformly the message of the disconcerting reports by the royal authorities in the various localities. In other words, the arguments with which it had formerly been possible to pacify the people's discontent with their material conditions were losing their force. Poverty and hunger hastened the collapse of ideological authorities which had already been shattered. The clergy, the "judicious" [*bien-pensants*], and the "wise" [*les sages*] called for submission and branded opposition [as wicked]; but life insistently and stubbornly demanded opposition. And inasmuch as these attempts to persuade and reassure were based on the broad tenets of a world-view inherited from the

Middle Ages, their very foundations proved, in the last resort, to have been shattered. The importance of these unanimous testimonies to the growing tenacity of the people in the seventeenth century in the face of religious as well as secular exhortation must not be underestimatted. The people were as yet incapable of opposing any new system of ideas to the old, but the old was steadily losing its hold over them. In order to maintain obedience, ever-increasing physical force was necessary, to compensate for the catastrophic decline in the influence of religion and of ideology generally as a factor in the social behavior of the masses.

In this context it is necessary to say a few words about the Huguenots. We have found comparatively little direct information about the connection of the Huguenots with the peasant and plebeian uprisings. The information we do have is, however, quite specific: [such connection as there is] has nothing to do with the religious inclinations of the insurgents and even less with religious fanaticism; it is simply a matter of practical ties between the Huguenot party and some of the movements. The intendant La Fosse, for example, asserts that the majority of the insurgent peasants in Angoumois and Saintonge in 1636 had previously participated in the Huguenot movement and were allied with it. Although we can uncover almost no traces of Huguenot ideology in the peasant and plebeian uprisings, we cannot overlook the fact that they broke out primarily in the very provinces which had earlier been the arena of the Huguenot movement: in the south and south-west of France, in parts of the west, and in Normandy to the north. Is this overlapping accidental? Of course not. But it suggests that in the past as well, the specifically religious side of Huguenotism was not nearly its most important side. It could, as we can see, recede or virtually disappear; and then the social basis would move to the forefront. The popular uprisings of the 1630's and 1640's brought to the fore what, for a century, had constituted the essence of Huguenotism, though it had been hidden under a religious garb and had been forced into the protective disguise of a church-party organization. A mass movement of social protest arose among the French people at the beginning of the sixteenth century. But because it was a spontaneous movement, a Calvinist organization was easily superimposed upon it, subjecting it to alien leadership, first by the bourgeoisie, then by the nobility and the feudal aristocracy. A hundred years later, with the disintegration of the noble and feudal-aristocratic superstructures (the Edict of Grace of 1629 was the beginning of the end of the Huguenots as a political party), the elemental power which had almost been harnessed by the stringent discipline of the Calvinist movement broke out once more in its pure form. That is the reason why we can find only traces of the ties between the popular movements and the Huguenots. The uprising at Montpellier in 1645 is an exception: there, as generally in Languedoc, the Huguenots left a deeper imprint on the popular movements.

Such were the motives, the social composition, the tactics, the organization, and the ideology of the urban risings from 1623 to 1648, described in the summary and somewhat haphazard fashion imposed by the material available. Yet this sketch enables us to form a judgment as to the nature of the "plebeian opposition" in the French town of the seventeenth century.

THE ENGLISH REVOLUTION, 1640–1660 *

Perez Zagorin †

I

The entrance of the enfranchised masses into politics as permanent participants; the permeation of the whole of social life by conflicting ideologies under whose banner the struggle for power is waged; a gi-

* While opposition to government in the first half of the seventeenth century led in France to rebellion, it led in England to full-fledged revolution. Professor Zagorin (University of Rochester) presents some of the reasons for regarding the "Great Rebellion"—as it was called by contemporaries—as the first major revolution in modern European history, and goes on to discuss two vital questions: (1) what was its social basis? (2) by what steps did it establish parliamentary government?

† Perez Zagorin, "The English Revolution, 1640–1660," *Journal of World History,* 2 (1955), pp. 668–676, 681, 895–900. Reprinted by permission of author and editor. For reasons of space, most of the footnotes have been omitted, as well as two sections of the article: a detailed discussion of the controversy over the rise of the gentry, and a substantial summary of the work of the revolution in religious and political thought. A fuller and more recent presentation of the "gentry" issue is given by Professor Zagorin in "The Social Interpretation of the English Revolution," *Journal of Economic History,* 19 (1959), pp. 376–401. The whole question of whether the English revolution was a "bourgeois" revolution, whether it was in fact basically social and economic in character, is in dispute. For a view contrary to Zagorin's, *see* J. H. Hexter, "Storm over the Gentry," reprinted in his *Reappraisals in History* (Evanston, Ill.: 1961). For a general review of the controversy *see* Christopher Hill, "Recent Interpretations of the Civil War," reprinted in his *Puritanism and Revolution* (New York: 1958).

gantic, continuing effort to install equality and democracy in all the institutions of society;—in these momentous facts we have learned to discern some of the principal features of our time. They are features which characterise a revolution. And, indeed, it is no exaggeration to call revolution the master theme in the history of the present age. A will to social transformation, self-conscious, planned, and guided by doctrine, has come to dominate in human affairs. At work for an interval in the revolution of the seventeenth century in England, and pressing forward without intermission since the revolution at the close of the eighteenth century in France, its scope is now world wide. Illusions it has bred in plenty, and tragic miscarriages mark its course. Yet its potency has but intensified as fresh groups and classes have come forth to infuse it with their interests and ideals. In the socialist and colonial revolutions of our own day, the movement of which it is the driving force has turned white hot. It is in a single continuous process, however, that these latter have succeeded the middle class revolutions of the preceding period.

Specialists are notoriously prone to partiality in favor of their own subject, and it may be that in viewing the English revolution of the two decades, 1640–1660, as the first great manifestation of the modern revolutionary temper, we shall be accused of assigning it an undeserved importance. What was there of much moment, we shall be asked, in a controversy between a seventeenth century king and his Parliament? And very likely we shall be told also that the character for compromise for which Englishmen are famed necessarily deprived their great rebellion of the significance we wish to see in it. Now that English politicians have frequently shown a conspicuous talent for adjusting sharp differences by compromise we shall readily admit. But this talent is a social acquirement gained over a long time, and an outcome of special circumstances in whose formation the events of the seventeenth century played an outstanding part. That it was yet in abeyance during the twenty years of revolution in England is clear, for the civil war between Crown and Parliament led on at last to the collapse of monarchy, the execution of the king on the charge of betraying the trust with which the people had invested him, and the establishment of a republic. These were extreme measures; nothing of politeness in them, but rather a gnashing of teeth and passionate hatred. And the consequence of the disintegration of royal power during the civil war, and of its abolition after the war's end, was the assumption of directing control by Parliament and its executive committees, the first time a great unitary state in

Europe was so ruled. Out of the controversy, therefore, as one result, Parliamentary government, and with it, the immense prestige it has long exercised, took their rise.

Moreover, while the struggle raged, thought passed beyond the trammels in which authority had long sought to confine it, and there occurred a discussion of social and political questions so intense and so wide ranging in scope as to be then almost without parallel. In the course of it, institutions came first to be looked upon in a frankly experimental spirit as things to be formed and reformed in accord with human intent. A new belief appeared that men could conquer happiness by the introduction of reason in social life. All grievances were aired, and all things brought under scrutiny—monarchy and church, the basis of political obligation, private property, liberty of conscience. Then, too, were commandingly formulated the complete theory of religious toleration and the utilitarian, civil liberty, and natural rights doctrines in whose subsequent triumphant progress thrones and altars were struck down. In the mind of one isolated visionary, even, a great flash of intuition issued in a plan for a cooperative communist republic that was without counterpart or equal until the rationalistic utopian socialism of the Enlightenment and the nineteenth century.

So vastly fruitful was the seventeenth century English revolution. And the significance which belongs to it may be grasped in another way if we compare it for a moment with several phenomena with which it has some affinity: the radicalism of the Anabaptist sects of the Reformation, the Dutch struggle for independence from Spain begun in the last quarter of the sixteenth century, and the social disturbances in other European states which were exactly contemporaneous with the English civil war and commonwealth.

The sectarian radicalism which was spurred on in Germany by Luther's break with the Roman church and which inspired the great peasant rebellion of 1525 and the communist experiment at Munster, represented a violent protest against feudalism. In the writings of Thomas Muenzer, who seems to have been a man of genius, it produced some social doctrines of much interest and acuteness. But the character of Anabaptism, when it forsook quietism and arrayed itself against the powers of the world, was overwhelmingly chiliastic. It looked with impatient eagerness for Christ's imminent second coming and sought to advance by its own efforts the reign of righteousness soon to be established under messianic auspices. In contrast, therefore, to the liberalism and radicalism which predominated in the English revolution, it lacked a political point of view and a political programme, and it soon exhausted and consumed itself in the intense flame of its chiliastic hopes. That is why it had not the long effect and influence of the ideas and institutional changes worked out in England between 1640 and 1660.

The example of the revolt of the Netherlands illustrates the unique significance of the English revolution in another way. The victory of the northern United Provinces may be regarded, under one aspect, as the earliest successful middle class revolution in Europe, and, as is well known, it cleared the road to the commercial and cultural eminence which the Dutch enjoyed throughout the seventeenth century. Yet we shall seek in vain in the Dutch rebellion for anything comparable to the great ferment of thought which agitated men's minds in the English revolution. Nor shall we find the Dutch invoking against Philip II of Spain the subversive doctrines which in England a few years later were to fill the anti-royalist and radical pamphlets of the 1640's. Though William of Orange and his followers upheld a right of resistance against their prince, they justified it chiefly on the ground that he had violated his obligations as a feudal suzerain by transgressing against the several customary and chartered privileges which the provinces had anciently possessed before the house of Habsburg entered into its Burgundian inheritance. They did not insist on a general right of subjects of their mere will to call a ruler to account and cashier him if they would. Neither was there anywhere even the dream of a universal franchise or an assertion of the natural right of every man to consent to the government under which he lives.

The conclusion we have been maintaining is as strongly enforced when we contrast the English revolution with the risings contemporaneous with it. There were five such: national-social rebellions against the Spanish monarchy in Catalonia, Portugal, and Naples; the peaceful, but nonetheless decisive, triumph of republicanism over the house of Orange in the United Provinces; and the Fronde, the last large effort in France before 1789 to curb the monarchy. None of these comes near possessing European significance; none was accompanied by any notable development in the realms either of thought or institutions. The Fronde, it is true, did stimulate considerable political discussion. But it does not seem to have produced a single fresh idea. Moreover, had either the princes or the Parlement won, they would not, unlike the English Houses of Parliament, have been capable of governing, and their victory would have entailed retrogression and, perhaps, anarchy for their country.

The English revolution alone, then, of these various social conflicts possesses an influence and significance which are European in scope and even world wide, if we consider that the libertarian ideas which it first announced continue, in a variety of forms, to figure in the struggles of the present day. And what we propose to do in the rest of this essay is to survey the social character of the English revolution, as scholars now debate it, and to look more closely at several of its aspects on which much of its importance depends.

II

While the occasion, or precipitating circumstances, of the English revolution is not in dispute among historians, its character, the nature of the social forces in opposition to one another, forms a subject of much recent discussion and disagreement. As to the former, the crisis which led to the summoning of the Long Parliament in November 1640 and to the outbreak of civil war less than two years later, had been decades preparing. During the reign of James I, and even more pronouncedly in that of his son, Charles I, Parliament, the Commons especially, had been challenging the king's traditional right under his prerogative of exercising supremacy in the determination of public policy. This challenge was itself an effect of the antagonism which the king's measures increasingly evoked. The imposition of a rigid conformity to ceremonies in the Church, a growing effort by the ecclesiastical authorities to exalt the episcopal order as divinely established, and the suspicion of a secret Catholic influence at court, had excited strong resistance in Parliament and roused the anti-clerical sentiments of the members and the dislike of Puritans. In foreign affairs, the king was believed to be designedly soft toward the Catholic powers and weakly unaggressive on behalf of the Protestant ones. In their opposition, the Houses had refused the financial support which the king called upon them to provide, and he was, in consequence, necessitated to raise money in non-Parliamentary ways by imposing of his sole will such taxes as ship money, a power which the judges held to be a legal exercise of the royal prerogative. The levying of ship money, and other vexatious financial expedients to which the king resorted, in turn brought dangerous protests in both Parliament and the country that the monarch was invading the liberty and property of the subject. So unmanageable did Parliament become, and so aggravated were the crown's relations with it, that from 1629 on, the king resolved to govern without summoning that body. For eleven years no Parliament met, and during this period, all the royal measures which had provoked such antagonism were more forcefully executed than before. Then in 1639, the crisis occurred. The government had attempted to impose the Liturgy of the Church of England upon the Scots, many of whom were Presbyterians and greatly under the influence of their zealous and unbending ministers. To the Presbyterians, the Anglican liturgy was a piece of popery, a graven Baal to which they would never bow the knee, and Scotland rose in rebellion. The king was now forced to convene Parliament, for only from Parliament could he obtain the money and the national support he required to put down the Scottish insurrection. When Parliament met in April 1640, however, it refused to take any steps against the Scots until the king redressed the grievances of which it complained, and it was dissolved after only three weeks. But the monarch's position was now so desperate that he could do nothing without his Parliament, whatever its demands might be, and he had no choice but to convene it once more. The Long Parliament began its sitting on 3 November 1640, and at once proceeded to take those steps whose final effect was to tear supremacy from the king and vest it in the Houses. A detested royal policy, then, against which opposition had risen to a climax by 1640, and the crisis of the Scottish rebellion–these are what furnished the occasion and the opportunity for the revolutionary Long Parliament.

But if the events which brought on the revolution seem clear enough, its social character is a more difficult problem. The matter is relatively uncomplicated so long as we speak of the king and of Parliament and limit ourselves to the constitutional and religious issues which divided them. But this, acceptable as it may be, does not advance our understanding as far as we should like. Most historians, irrespective of their particular point of view, have learned to analyse revolutions as great class battles in which state power is at stake and on whose outcome opposed ways of organising social life depend; and in the French and Russian revolutions, which provide two outstanding instances for this kind of analysis, there is ample confirmation of its correctness. What needs to be made clear, therefore, is whether the English revolution is best explicable in similar terms; whether, that is to say, the Royalists and Parliamentarians each represent the interests of distinct and opposing social classes or coalitions of such, and whether the religious and political and other doctrines of the time are significantly related to the social position of their several exponents. In other words, in what way is the great English civil war a bourgeois revolution?

That the revolution lacked any definite social character, that it was not, at any rate, a social conflict, is the view we ought to note first, since it is this to which S. R. Gardiner, the great historian of seventeenth century England, lent the weight of his authority. In an opening page of his narrative of the civil war, Gardiner declared that, unlike the French revolution, the struggle was not between classes, for there were noblemen, gentlemen, yeomen, and townsmen on both sides. Such also is the opinion of another great scholar, Professor G. M. Trevelyan, who calls the conflict one, not of classes, but of ideas. This view, however, is too simple to be convincing. In every revolution, one may find numerous instances of members of the same classes taking opposite sides or remaining neutral, and this because of the multiplicity of motives from which men act. The historian knows that he cannot encompass the variety of these motives in a formula, and thinks himself under no necessity to do so. He feels on firm ground, nonetheless, if the evidence enables him to distinguish between opposing class interests and ways of organising social life which will triumph or fail in the victory of one party or the other. Moreover, in seeking the social meaning of the war, he does not, of course, intend to deny the leading role which ideas play in the actions of men or to treat them as mere epiphenomena, shadow-puppets controlled by some over-riding economic necessity. He wishes only to see ideas in their setting, functioning in relation to the social changes which they may either hinder or promote. Nor does the historian suppose that if he succeeds in grasping the social basis of the revolution, he will have thereby exhausted its significance. Religious doctrines and organisation, political thought, and literary activity, for example, all possess a real existence of their own whose intrinsic interest is enhanced rather than diminished when they are illumined by an account of the interaction between them and the environing conflict.

But these considerations are merely qualifications which all historians must make when pursuing their inquiry into the nature of revolutionary struggles, and they do not, of course, militate against the validity of the inquiry itself. The fact is that Gardiner was uninterested in social history and had scarcely any conception of it, while Trevelyan's concern has been more with the illustration of contemporary manners, types, and customs, in the style of the well known third chapter of Lord Macaulay's *History of England,* than with the analysis of the changing social structure in the sixteenth and seventeenth centuries. Confined to their standpoint, we either answer inadequately, or do not answer at all, many questions of importance: why, for example, Puritanism was more prevalent in the towns, why the clothing districts supported Parliament, why Parliament abolished feudal tenures but left base tenures intact, why the radical movements appeared and made the sort of protest they did. The proof of the insufficiency of the view of Gardiner and Trevelyan is that questions of this order, which had little or no interest for them, are the very ones which have for some years been increasingly engaging the attention and labor of other scholars.

Passing now to a brief account of recent efforts at a social interpretation of the revolution, one view appears to dominate here, though it is not unanimously accepted nor are its details entirely agreed upon or very extensively worked out even by those who support it. On this view, the genesis of the civil war is to be found in the sharpening struggle between, on the one side, the most economically advanced forces in the country, whose development forms the principal theme of English economic and social history during the century 1540–1640, and, on the other side, a mercantile group closely linked to the crown and a conservative court and aristocracy variously characterised as semi-feudal or, at any rate, as economically unprogressive. Within the former were to be found, for example, such merchants as were closely connected with industry, like the clothiers associated with the textile manufacture in the provinces; many yeomen and small freeholders; and a new lesser gentry, the ranks of which were recruited from a variety of sources, whose members conducted agriculture as a business and who were alert to exploit the mineral resources on their lands and to utilise opportunities for profitable investment in industrial, commercial, and colonial enterprise. Within the latter were included merchants dependent for their profits on grants of monopoly trading privileges from the crown; mercantile financiers who were money lenders to the king and in receipt of lucrative appointments in various branches of the royal revenue; office holders and courtiers deriving incomes from crown patents; and a peerage and aristocracy, or greater gentry, declining in wealth owing to inefficient land management in the face of changing economic conditions, extravagance, and debt.

Several instances of this interpretation may be cited. Professor Nef, for example, has contended that between 1540–1640, England experienced an industrial revolution which laid the basis for its subsequent economic primacy and brought fresh social elements to the fore who were unwilling to acquiesce in the traditional controls imposed by the state. He has concluded that . . .

. . . the rapid expansion of large-scale enterprise and industrial output . . . was helping to undermine royal authority. The attempts of [royal] ministers to control industry in the teeth of the early industrial revolution, helped to produce an economic conflict between the Stuart kings and some of their most powerful subjects, the leading town merchants and the improving landlords. Together with the religious and political conflicts described by Gardiner and other historians, this economic conflict, with its industrial origins, brought about the constitutional crisis of the seventeenth century. The influence of industrial upon constitutional history was more positive and probably stronger than the influence of constitutional upon industrial history.[1]

Similarly, Mr. L. Stone has declared that

Fundamentally, the growing hostility to the system of control at the end of the [sixteenth] century was the sympton of the rise of a new class of gentry, lawyers, small merchants and entrepreneurs, retailers and middlemen, hitherto excluded from the major benefits of the economic system and hampered in their activity by the official policy—both of which they were finally to sweep away by force in 1640. For if the Elizabethan and early Stuart system reserved its richest rewards for a limited number of courtiers and great merchant financiers, the economic developments of the century nevertheless brought in their trail the rise of a broad-based lesser *bourgeoisie* who progressively strengthened their hold upon the national wealth and their influence in the Lower House of Parliament. Half a century had elapsed without any serious rioting or rebellion by the poor and the fear of social unrest had consequently faded. Foreign invasion had so often threatened without result that even that menace had now grown stale. Gratitude for the benefits of the regime now therefore gave way to a spirit of criticism of its more unpopular features. The ring was cleared of interference by the poor or by the Spaniard, and the battle between the conservative aristocracy and the new middle-classes was engaged in earnest.[2]

As one aspect of this general point of view, several scholars have endeavoured to depict the ruling group against whom the civil war was waged as a "semi-feudal aristocracy, the successors in social position and political power . . . of the feudal class which had ruled in England since the Norman Conquest," having explained that by feudalism is meant "a form of society in which agriculture is the basis of the economy and in which political power is monopolised by a class of landowners."[3]

[1] J. U. Nef, *Industry and Government in France and England, 1540–1640* (Philadephia: 1940), p. 149.

[2] L. Stone, "State Control in Sixteenth Century England," *Economic History Review,* XVII, n. 2 (1947), p. 120. For similar views, cf. Christopher Hill, *The English Revolution* (2nd ed., London: 1949), ch. 1; M. Dobb, *Studies in the Development of Capitalism* (New York: 1947), pp. 170–171, and M. Ashley, *England in the Seventeenth Century* (London: 1952), pp. 78–80.

[3] Christopher Hill and E. Dell, *The Good Old Cause* (London: 1950), p. 19; Christopher Hill, *The English Revolution,* p. 6.

They have not succeeded, however, in gaining the assent to this opinion even of those students with whom they are in accord in other respects. That there were important survivals of the feudal age in Tudor and Stuart England is unquestioned; and while some, such as wardships, have been studied,[4] others, such as the manorial courts through which a large part of landlords' power was exercised over many thousands of people, have been relatively neglected. These courts, and associated manorial institutions which profoundly affected the agricultural population and often townsmen as well, all require further investigation if a deeper understanding of seventeenth century social life is to be won. But it is doubtful, nevertheless, whether there is any gain in clarity in speaking of landlords as a "semi-feudal aristocracy," and Professor Tawney's stricture seems warranted when he writes: "If the word 'feudal' refers merely to territorial influence, it draws no dividing line between Royalists and Parliamentarians, for such influence was exercised by both. If it is used, as it should be, in a more precise sense, to describe a class dependent wholly or mainly, like the French *noblesse* before 1789, on the revenue from seigneurial rights, it is a solecism; for unless the rights in question be interpreted to include all or most payments from tenants to landlords, evidence of the existence of such a class in the England of Charles I is still to seek." [5] . . .

Despite the limits to our present knowledge, the character of the revolution as a social conflict has not been placed in doubt. It is not the fact of such a conflict which is disputed, but its precise nature. Though no class differences have been found to distinguish the Royalist from the Parliamentarian members of the Long Parliament, it is recognised that the M.P.'s were by no means characteristic of the population; and such differences, operating on lower social levels, may have divided the mass of Parliamentary supporters from the Royalists as a whole. There is reason for thinking this to be the fact, and to account, for example, for the strength which Parliament's cause mustered in the towns and in the most economically advanced regions of the country. It is also clear that as the revolution developed, we see the independent action on behalf of their own interests of both urban and rural lower class groups, and the presence in the apparatus of local government of Parliamentarians

[4] Cf. J. B. Hurstfield, "The Revival of Feudalism in Early Tudor England," *History*, XXXVII, p. 130 (1952), and H. E. Bell, *An Introduction to the History and Records of the Court of Wards and Liveries* (Cambridge: 1953).

[5] R. H. Tawney, Introduction to D. Brunton and D. H. Pennington, *Members of the Long Parliament* (London: 1954), pp. xix-xx; and cf. the remarks of Messrs. Brunton and Pennington, *ibid.* pp. 179–180.

with lower social position than the gentlemen who had been conspicuous in the earlier 1640's. In any case, the victory of Parliament was decisive in turning the current of social life into a new channel where it could flow unhindered by the obstacles that had stood in its way before 1640. The older forms of state control were struck down, and after 1660 the government ceased to confer patents of monopoly and to intervene against enclosure. The aristocratic order survived, but in a new shape, for money far more than birth was now its basis. And Parliament itself became the instrument chiefly of landed capitalists, Whig and Tory both, and their connections and allies, whose interests the state now unswervingly pursued.

III

We come now to look more closely at some of the achievements of the English revolution, and first of all with respect to the establishment of Parliamentary government.

Little imagination is required to grasp the largeness of the task which Parliament confronted when it undertook to rule the country in the crisis of a civil war. The Houses were playing for the most terrible stakes. Were they to lose the war, the lives and fortunes of the leaders who had organised the opposition to the king would certainly be forfeit, while the penalties on all the more prominent Parliamentarians would also be heavy. Yet in 1640, Parliament was utterly without corporate experience as an executive body. Now it had all at once, and under the hardest of circumstances, to assume the functions of government which until then had been exercised by the king, the privy council, and a host of royal officials. That Parliament succeeded amidst many vicissitudes and difficulties in triumphing in the war and in governing the country is the strongest testimony of its capacity and of the absurdity of Charles I's policy in attempting to maintain it in its traditional tutelage to him and his ministers. As a result of this achievement, Parliamentary government was firmly established, surviving and flourishing even after the restoration of the Stuarts.

Early in its sitting, the Long Parliament enacted legislation which secured its independence of and control over the king and his councillors. The Triennial Act, passed in February 1641, required that there should be no interval of more than three years between Parliaments and created the machinery to effect this object. Legislation in May prohibited the dissolution of the Long Parliament without its own consent, and in July, the king's conciliar jurisdiction was taken away by the abolition of the Court of Star Chamber, the councils of the Marches of Wales and the North, and the Court of High Commission. Other acts prohibited the levying of tonnage and poundage without consent of Parliament and declared illegal the financial expedients such as ship money of which the king had made use before 1640. All these measures, which obtained the King's unwilling assent, remained on the statute book after 1660.

As the outbreak of civil war drew near, Parliament began the process of transforming itself into an executive. The great factor which enabled it to go forward to the solution of the problems of governing upon which the issue of victory or defeat depended was the presence in the House of Commons, where lay the heart of the resistance to the king, of members of the highest ability, some of whom possessed long Parliamentary experience. These were the men who framed the measures necessary for the prosecution of the war and steered them through the Commons. John Pym, for example, the leader of the House until his death in December 1643, had sat in every Parliament since 1621. So also had John Hampden, as much esteemed by his colleagues as was Pym. Sir Henry Vane the younger and Oliver St. John had not held seats before the Long Parliament, but both were eminently qualified to play a conspicuous role in the House and at once took rank among the most prominent members. Men such as Pym and Hampden, and other influential figures on Parliament's side, knew the procedure of the House and understood the art of committee work. They were living representatives of the earlier great struggles which Parliament had waged against the crown. They had seen the Commons seize the initiative in the 1620's, had helped win the Petition of Right, and had been one with Sir John Eliot in the impeachment of the Duke of Buckingham. They had taken part in the stormy scene in Charles I's last Parliament before 1640, when the Speaker of the House had been forcibly held in his chair to prevent an adjournment, while the members shouted their acclamation of resolutions against illegal taxation. They knew enough of the king to be confirmed in their distrust of him and were determined, if negotiations came, to negotiate with the king in strength and not in weakness.

The committee system was the method Parliament employed to carry on its government. The Houses had long been accustomed to establish committees for the consideration of various special subjects, and these were, of course, formed when the Long Parliament met. But for long, however, there was no leading body entrusted by Parliament with powers that amounted to a centralised direction of affairs, nor were there in the counties any appropriate and trustworthy organs through which the orders of Parliament could be carried out. The want of these was a serious obstacle to the conduct of the war and to the effective mobilisation of the extensive resources which the Houses had potentially at their disposal. The first approach to the establishment of a controlling body acting with broad powers was made early in July 1642 when it had become clear that war was imminent. At that time, the Houses concurred in the formation of a Committee of Safety consisting of fifteen persons, ten commoners and five peers, whose duty it would be "to take into . . . consideration whatsoever may concern the Safety of the Kingdom, the Defence of the Parliament, and the Preservation of the Peace of the Kingdom, and opposing any force that may be raised against Parliament; and to meet as often as they please." In pursuit of these objects, the Committee was expected to recommend measures and to carry out policies upon which Parliament had decided, though it was in the latter department that it was most active. It never became, however, what it was in germ, the executive head of the government. The Houses kept close watch upon it, and those leaders in the Commons, such as Sir Henry Vane the younger, who opposed any settlement with the king, were repeatedly critical of its inefficiency and of the too pacific attitude of the peers who were of its membership. After nineteen months, the Committee of Safety was abolished and replaced by a new body which did at last concentrate in itself the powers necessary to make it the chief executive instrument of Parliamentary government.

Early in 1643, while the problem of effective central control still remained to be solved, the basic outline of the form assumed by local government until the Restoration was laid down in measures in whose conception and passage Pym appears to have taken the chief part. By ordinances respectively of February and March 1643, the levying of a weekly assessment and the sequestration of royalists' lands was provided for, and in fulfillment of these ends it was ordered that committees should be established in every county and principal town. Thus were erected the county committees to which in course of time were assigned the principal tasks of administration in the counties, including the levying and collection of taxes. Cumbersome these committees certainly were, and they offered, too, ample opportunity for financial corruption and the pursuit of private vendettas and revenges. They were commonly not very efficient in their working, and frequently caused much heart ache to those, friend and foe alike, who had to deal with them. Nevertheless, the system of county committees was the best that could be devised, for it was adaptable to a wide variety of purposes and had the advantage of being able to draw into its work a large number of persons. Moreover, because it was based on the tried and customary method of local government by the men of the neighbourhood, it was, on the whole, inoffensive to public sentiment. Despite the multiplicity of tasks which the committees discharged, they had no judicial jurisdiction, and quarter sessions of the Justices of the Peace continued to be held, as did the assizes of the judges on eyre, once the country was at peace. With the successive struggles and alterations on Parliament's side which occurred after the civil war and the disruption of the Parliamentary coalition, the personnel of the county committees was frequently changed, men of lower social station being often appointed and sometimes, as in some of the Welsh counties, former Royalists. They remained, however, the basis of local government until the return of Charles II, and succeeded, in the main, notwithstanding their deficiencies, "in harnessing to the new republican governments the traditional forces of county society."

It was in February 1644, by the establishment of the Committee of Both Kingdoms, that a true executive, even the "germ of the modern Cabinet system," was at last created and given full command of affairs. The Committee was a consequence of certain clauses of the treaty against the king into which Parliament had entered with the Scots in the previous November. To maintain the unity of the two nations and facilitate their cooperation in the war, the treaty provided that no peace should be made with the king except by consent of both kingdoms or committees appointed to act on their behalf, and that any differences arising between the Scots and Parliament should be mutually adjusted by them or their representatives. Thereafter the Scots dispatched commissioners to London to act for them in dealing with the English Parliament, and in the latter, in turn, a proposal was put forward to appoint a committee for consultation with the Scots. This proposal was finally developed amidst intrigue and controversy into an ordinance inspired by the younger Sir Henry Vane and Oliver St. John, in which Parliament superseded the old Committee of Safety and appointed a new body of twenty-one persons, of whom fourteen were commoners and seven peers, entrusting them with the direction of the war in cooperation with the Scottish commissioners who were also to be members. By this ordinance, authority was conferred upon the Committee not only to act for the Houses in all transactions with the Scots, but also "to advise, consult, order, and direct, concerning the carrying on and managing of the

War . . . and likewise . . . to hold good Correspondency and Intelligence with Foreign States. . . ." As many of the members had expressed the fear that a body with such wide powers would escape Parliamentary control, the Committee was denied any authority to treat concerning a cessation of arms or a peace without express direction from the Houses, and a term of only three months was set for its continuance. Moreover, a provision in the original draft of the ordinance imposing an oath of secrecy upon the Committee was struck out on the ground that all members of Parliament were entitled to information in anything that concerned the state. Most of these limitations, however, were temporary. In May 1644, the Committee's life expired, but it was then continued without term of time, despite strong opposition in the Upper House; and in the following July, the earlier prohibition against an oath of secrecy was lifted, and the members were required to swear not to divulge any of the Committee's debates or resolutions.

The energy with which the Committee of Both Kingdoms used its authority in the conduct of the war and the breadth of the subjects with which it concerned itself may be studied in the *Calendars of State Papers Domestic,* in whose pages from 1644 on its deliberations occupy for some time the chief place. We need not follow its activities. It is sufficient to note that after the Committee's foundation, it appears to have been the prototype of every executive body which succeeded it at the head of the revolutionary governments. Dissolved in January 1648 in order to end the connection with the Scottish commissioners, it was replaced by a purely English body, the Committee of Derby House. When the king was executed and the commonwealth proclaimed, the Commons, which was all that remained of Parliament in the new English republic, proceeded to create a council of state as its chief executive organ and to give it powers even broader than those enjoyed by the Committee of Both Kingdoms. All through the 1650's, under both the commonwealth and the protectorate, a succession of councils of state exercised the leading functions of administration.

In this way Parliament learned the mysteries of government. The large number of committees set up during the revolutionary decades with executive jurisdiction over special subjects gave it wide knowledge of many problems and the power to deal with them; while by means of such bodies as the councils of state, it controlled the whole apparatus of administration. Despite the fact that Parliament lost its executive functions at the Restoration, the effect wrought upon it by the experiences of the revolutionary years was of permanent imporance. It had taken greedily to the business of governing, and the knowledge it had acquired could not be lost, for "the corporate consciousness of a great body like the House of Commons," it has been well remarked, "is superior to the shocks of dissolutions and intermissions. Records, traditions, recollections survive, and are handed on from one generation to another." In addition, the legislation of 1641 which deprived the king of his most important prerogative powers remained operative after the Restoration. As the ease with which James II was overthown in 1688 shows, Parliamentary government had won. Never after 1660 could the crown act successfully in defiance of the two Houses.

THE ENGLISH REVOLUTION AND THE BROTHERHOOD OF MAN *

Christopher Hill †

I

The Revolution which began in 1640 marked a decisive turning point in English history. It was also an event of European significance. The execution of Charles I in 1649 in the name of the people of England led all European countries to sever diplomatic relations with the English republic: the Tsar of Russia seized the occasion to deprive English merchants of the exclusive trading privileges by virtue of which they had tried to reduce Russia to colonial status. Foreign intervention on behalf of the old regime was prevented by the absorption of all the great powers in the Thirty Years' War, and the war between France and

* The English Revolution is all too often treated, in contrast to the French Revolution of 1789 and the Russian of 1917, as a purely national event. But, as Christopher Hill (Balliol College, Oxford) shows in the following essay, it was an event with international ramifications. And at least some of the revolutionaries believed themselves to be acting in no narrow cause, but in the cause of mankind.

† Christopher Hill, "The English Revolution and the Brotherhood of Man," *Science and Society,* 18 (1954), pp. 289–309. Footnotes have been omitted. Reprinted with permission of the editor. For additional information on connections between the English and other revolutions of the mid-seventeenth century see R. B. Merriman, *Six Contemporaneous Revolutions* (Oxford: 1938). Some stimulating suggestions may be found in the minutes of a 1957 symposium on "Seventeenth Century Revolutions," printed in *Past and Present,* No. 13 (April, 1958), pp. 63–72.

Spain which continued until December 1659. The English Revolution, unlike the French Revolution of 1789 and the Russian Revolution of 1917, was able to work out its problems free from direct foreign interference. This helps to account for the "lack of bitterness" in the Revolution, of which English historians are apt to boast and which too many attribute to the virtuous English character. But the possibility of foreign intervention was always present in the minds of the leaders of either side in the civil war: and the speed with which Charles II was hurried back to England in 1660 sprang partly from fear that the Peace of the Pyrenees might make possible a conjunction of France and Spain to restore the king as an absolute ruler and not as a parliamentary monarch.

Many of the leaders, and still more of the rank and file, thought of the Revolution which had begun in England as an international event. The Parliament which met in 1640, Samuel Hartlib thought, would "lay the cornerstone of the world's happiness." Hartlib himself aimed at "the reformation of the whole world" and others shared his consciousness of responsibilities to other peoples. It is the object of this article briefly to consider the international repercussions of the Revolution, and to illustrate the sentiments of internationalism to which it gave rise.

II

Previous history had made it inevitable that the overthrow of the monarchy and the ecclesiastical hierarchy in England should be of international significance. The rise of capitalist relations all over Europe had profoundly shaken feudal society. The struggles associated with the Protestant reformation are an expression of this crisis. In Spain and Italy Protestantism and the bourgeoisie were defeated: both countries entered on a long period of economic stagnation. In France, after a bitter civil war, the Edict of Nantes registered the failure of the Huguenots to capture state power: by recognizing them as a religious minority within the state it deprived them of their political allies and soon reduced them to impotence. In England, Scandinavia, and parts of Germany, rulers allied with the more conservative protestants first to plunder the church and then to protect themselves against peasant revolt. Only in the Netherlands did a thorough-going bourgeois revolt, under Calvinist leadership, succeed in overthrowing the old order on a national scale (as distinguished from the victories in Geneva and the Swiss cities). For a century after their victory the Dutch bourgeoisie was the richest in Europe.

From the death of Edward VI (1553) the monarchy in England adopted a conservative social policy. It called a halt to the reformation and proceeded to consolidate the episcopal church under its own control. Henceforwards, whilst one section of the bourgeoisie was bought off with economic privileges, a steadily growing section began to call for a radical completion of the reformation in England and for a new expansionist foreign policy. The abolition of the episcopal hierarchy would have meant the overthrow of the feudal state's main instrument of thought-control, the abolition of ecclesiastical courts would have removed a serious obstacle to free capitalist development, and its replacement by a presbyterian or congregational discipline through which the local bourgeoisie would be able to impose an ideology of hard work on the lower classes; the confiscation of church property would accelerate the accumulation of capital. The radical Puritan programme was, and was recognized by contemporaries to be, a demand for a transfer of political power. Said Archbishop Bancroft of this programme: "the [Norman] Conquest brought not such an alteration. Six kings' reigns of Parliaments would not bring this platform to any tolerable government."

"The chief use" of the clergy, said a public servant who was to be secretary of state to Charles I from 1625 to 1639, "is now the defence of our church, and therein of our state." The church was co-extensive with the state, or rather with society. The great Puritan leader, John Preston, in a sermon preached before the King in 1626, declared: "We cannot do God a more acceptable turn than to help his churches, through for the present they seem to be under the cloud of his anger." By "the churches" Preston meant those sections of the population in other countries, whether they controlled state power or not, who shared his general outlook. The phrase covered both the Dutch Republic and the Huguenot minority in France. "We forget the misery of the Church in other places," said Richard Sibbes, another leading Puritan divine; ". . . they pray, and call upon us, as far as Prague, as far as Heidelberg, as far as France, that we would take notice of their afflictions."

The radicals in England saw their own struggle against a background of civil war and persecution in most countries of the continent. An international conflict was taking place from which, they felt, England could hold aloof only at her peril. "If any of the churches be swallowed up," said Preston in the sermon I have just quoted, "you know that is a thing that cannot be recalled; and therefore let us do our best, and do it in time." Preaching again at court a year later,

Preston returned to the charge: "When the enemy is assaulting the Churches afar off, he is even then striking at the root of this church and commonwealth. . . . Do we not see the whole body of those that profess the truth are besieged round about through Christendom? . . . Are not present enemies not only stirred up, but united together, and we disjoined to resist them? . . . Are not many branches of the church cut off already, and more in hazard?"

There were many attempts to found a protestant international, at first with the blessing of the English government. In 1614 a Scottish minister was arrested in France, who was carrying to a Huguenot synod a proposal from James I for the union of all protestant churches under the leadership of the king of England. In the next year the famous theologian Paraeus of Heidelberg published his *Irenicon* which aimed at uniting Lutherans and Calvinists under the patronage of the kings of Denmark and England. The Elizabethan and early Jacobean governments regarded "the protestant interest" as the English interest. In 1605 the great-nephew of Secretary Cecil could write to his great-uncle about William of Orange's daughter, widow of a Huguenot nobleman: "She is a foreigner, but protestant, and so depending of our state." But after the outbreak of the Thirty Years' War in 1618 the English government recoiled from the idea of taking the lead of a European protestant party. In 1622 the works of Paraeus were publicly burnt in England. Charles I gave no support to John Dury's attempt to revive the cause of protestant unity in the sixteen-thirties: he had to look to the opposition. And so the European ideological struggle became an issue in internal English politics.

Men like Preston and Sibbes and their followers saw a vast and co-ordinated Catholic conspiracy, aiming at the suppression of protestantism and political liberty. Against this conspiracy the Dutch, the Huguenots, the Bohemian rebels, the Elector Palatine and Gustavus Adolphus were in the most literal sense fighting the battles of their English brethren. It was with burning shame that such patriots saw the supine or hostile attitude of their government whilst these great issues were at stake. The governments of James I and Charles I pursued a timid foreign policy because they lacked money; but their financial difficulties arose from their inability to pursue a policy at home or abroad, of which the tax-paying classes approved. James and Charles had an entirely different scale of values from that which put the welfare of protestantism, the commercial and industrial interests of England, first. James I advised his son to count rebellion against any other prince a crime against himself; yet many protestant subjects of catholic rulers had no choice between rebellion and emigration, or death.

So the religious disputes over foreign policy were not abstract theological disagreements, or differing warmths of sentiment: they were the expression of opposed philosophies of life. The one, the royalist, put hierarchy, degree, social subordination first: kings are natural allies against their subjects, trade and industry exist for the benefit of the landed aristocracy and of the royal exchequer; a national religion is a useful means of preserving unity and obedience. The other, the parliamentarian, wanted above all to see the national wealth increased (in the first instance, through the enrichment of traders, privateers, and those producing for the market); it was utilitarian, not afraid of drawing on the energy and self-confidence of the unprivileged: in a negative sense it was egalitarian. It saw the international struggle not as a conflict of protestant rebels against catholic kings, but of God's cause versus the devil's, of conscience against authoritarian tyranny. It saw a regime which maintained itself by persecution facing one which trusted the independence of free men. And Charles Stuart was on the side of Anti-Christ.

III

The Dutch Revolt played the same part in politics and thought as the Spanish civil war in the nineteen-thirties, only for a longer period. A regiment was recruited among English catholic emigrés to help to suppress the revolt: all the chaplains were Jesuits, and Guy Fawkes, who tried to blow up the Houses of Parliament in 1605, was one of its officers. On the rebel side there were rarely fewer than 5,000 English volunteers. Many of these "volunteers" were mercenaries; many dubious characters took advantage of continental wars to make piratical raids on Spanish colonies in America: it is easy to make jokes about the importance of plunder and piracy in the early history of protestantism. But that is of the essence of the situation. We cannot draw rigid lines between those who acted out of religious idealism and those who acted out of economic calculation. Which prevailed when the merchants of London sent £500,000 to the rebel Dutch out of their own pocket—more than a year's government revenue? When in 1588 the City was asked to provide 15 ships and 5,000 men for defense against the Spanish Armada, the City fathers pleaded for two days to think it over; they returned with an offer of 30 ships and 10,000 men. It was private enterprise which beat the Armada almost in the government's despite: the fight for American colonies, from Drake to the Providence Island Company, was undertaken by private enterprise in face of government disapproval.

In the sixteen-twenties and thirties a great campaign developed in England to send help to protestant Bohemia in the Thirty Years' War. The lead was taken by Thomas Scott, a minister who had been silenced for his Puritan views. In his pamphlets he attacked the influential Spanish ambassador, defended Puritans and Parliaments, and pleaded for an alliance with the Dutch Republic against Spain and Austria. His support, we are told, came not only from "the meaner sort that were zealous for the cause of religion" but also from "all men of judgment." To such men, our source continues, the battle of White Mountain seemed the greatest blow the church of God had received since the reformation. They feared it would lead in the end to the subversion of protestantism in England. All men that had any religion looked to the meeting of Parliament for a remedy.

Such men looked to Parliament. But Charles I tried to rule without summoning Parliament, whilst letting down repeatedly those whom the Commons regarded as natural allies—the Elector Palatine, La Rochelle, Gustavus Adolphus. When the latter marched into Germany and routed the Hapsburgs, the government, far from sharing popular joy, issued an order forbidding gazettes to print news of Swedish successes. Shortly afterwards newspapers were prohibited altogether: the news for which public opinion was hungry could only be spread by ballads, whose popularity increased rapidly. But soon the news ceased to be good. In 1634 Gustavus Adolphus was killed in action. Thomas Beedome expressed prevalent feelings of guilt in praying that:

> This be the latest loss we may sustain
> And that no more of Heaven's great champions fall,
> Through our default, to so sad funeral.

Charles I, whose "default" it mainly was, so far from feeling guilty, offered Spain a military alliance against Sweden and the Netherlands. Diplomatic relations were established with the Papacy for the first time since the reformation. "These priestly policies of theirs," wrote Milton in 1641, "having thus exhausted our domestic forces, have gone the way also to leave us naked of our firmest and faithfullest neighbours abroad, by disparaging and alienating from us all protestant princes and commonwealths; who are not ignorant that our prelates, and as many as they can infect, account them no better than a sort of sacrilegious and puritanical rebels, preferring the Spaniard, our deadly enemy, before them."

But already as Milton wrote the revolution was changing the scene.

IV

When civil war began between King and Parliament in 1642, there were many Englishmen and Scots who had had much experience of warfare. The Scottish army of the Covenant was officered almost entirely by men who had served under Gustavus Adolphus. Among officers in the English parliamentary army, Essex, Fairfax, Skippon and Monck had seen service in the Thirty Years' War: individual Dutch, Swedish, German and Huguenot soldiers fought on Parliament's side.

Many of the Parliamentary leaders stressed the international aspects of their cause, and its international obligations. Thus in September 1642 Pym, urging the two houses to unite closely with Scotland in matters of church government, reminded them that "Jesuitical and prelatical faction" which had dominated Charles I's government had not only caused a crisis in England but had "threatened ruin . . . to all . . . the reformed Churches." The peace propositions which Parliament offered to the King at York (June 1642), Oxford (February 1643), Uxbridge (November 1644) all demanded an alliance with the Dutch Republic and other protestant states against the designs of the Pope and his adherents, and for the recovery of the Palatinate. In 1643 General Leslie, commanding the Scottish army, was reported as saying "what a glorious thing it would be . . . if we manage to drive the Catholics out of England and follow them to France, and in imitation of the late King of Sweden unite with those of our religion there, and plant our religion in Paris by agreement or by force, and thence go to Rome, drive out Antichrist and burn the town that disseminates superstition."

Even stronger views were expressed by secondary figures. The Rev. John Goodwin, for instance, in a pamphlet published in the third month of the Civil War, reminded his readers that "the action wherein the church and people of God in the land are now engaged" was of great concern "to all the Saints of God" in all the reformed churches. If their cause prospered "it will be the riches, strength and increase of them"; "the heat and warmth and living influence thereof shall pierce through many kingdoms great and large, as France, Germany, Bohemia,

Hungary, Poland, Denmark, Sweden, with many others." The Rev. Hugh Peters, in a sermon preached in 1645 before the Houses of Parliament, the Assembly of Divines, the Lord Mayor and Alderman of London, declared: "Methinks I see Germany lifting up her lumpish shoulder, and the thin-cheeked Palatinate looking out, a prisoner of hope; Ireland breathing again, that not only lay bedrid, but the pulse beating deathward: the overawed French peasant studying his long-lost liberty, the Netherlanders looking back upon their neighbouring England, who cemented their walls with their blood, and bought their freedom with many, many thousands of good old Elizabeth shillings. Indeed, methinks, all Protestant Europe seems to get new colour in her cheeks."

Parliament's complete victory in the civil war gave its supporters a new consciousness of a mission. Milton's defense of regicide was read in the Netherlands, France, Germany, Sweden, Greece. Hugh Peters was reported (by a hostile witness) to have preached a sermon before the Houses of Parliament on December 22nd, 1648, in which he declared "This army must root up monarchy, not only here, but in France and other kingdoms round about; this is to bring you out of Egypt: this Army . . . must dash the powers of the earth to pieces."

The same sense of destiny was expressed by Andrew Marvell in 1650 when he wrote of Oliver Cromwell in his *Horatian Ode*:

> As Caesar he ere long to Gaul,
> To Italy as Hannibal
> And to all states not free
> Shall climacteric be.

Such sentiments came closer to reality when repeated on Spanish territory in 1651 by Admiral Blake, commanding the strongest fleet in the world. He was reported as saying in the public square of Cadiz that monarchy was a kind of government the world was weary of; he believed that all countries would soon annihilate tyranny and become republics. "England had done so already; France was following in her wake; and as the natural gravity of the Spaniards rendered them somewhat slower in their operations, he gave them ten years for the revolution in their country." Such words spoken by such a man in such a place were ominous indeed.

V

So much for theory. What influence did the revolution have on other countries in practice? It has been noted that 1648, like 1848, was a year of revolutions. Professor R. B. Merriman dealt with them in a book entitled *Six Contemporaneous Revolutions* (Oxford, 1938). His six were in England, France, Catalonia, Portugal (these last two from 1640 onwards) Naples (1647–48) and the Netherlands (1650). He might have aded a seventh, the revolt in 1648 of the Ukrainian Cossacks against the Polish Government. Oliver Cromwell is said to have congratulated their leader, Bogdan Khmelnitsky, on his victories over the Polish gentry. There is little evidence of any influence from England on events in Catalonia or Portugal, both Catholic countries. The representative of the Portuguese government identified himself with the King's cause in the civil war. Only pressure from Blake's fleet, and their mutual hostility to Spain, brought Portugal to establish diplomatic relations with England: a treaty signed in 1654 gave English merchants a favoured position in Portugal and her Empire. For the revolt led by Masaniello in Naples there appears to have been more sympathy among the English revolutionaries. A speaker at a meeting in London in November 1647 said "The same business we are upon is perfected in Naples, for if any person stand up for monarchy there, he is immediately hanged at his door." Anthony Ascham's *Discourse, wherein is examined what is particularly Lawfull during the Confusions and Revolutions of Government* (1648) drew on Neapolitan experience; and in 1650 an English translation of Alessandro Giraffi's *The Revolution of Naples* was published.

On the French Fronde, on the other hand, the influence of the English Revolution was great. The Parlement of Paris consciously imitated claims put forward by the English Parliament in 1640–41. In 1650 or 1651 Sir Henry Vane, one of the most influential figures in the government of the English republic, was sent over to make contact with Cardinal de Retz, the Frondeur leader. Vane carried a letter from Cromwell praising De Retz's "defence of the public liberty." The Cardinal, who was most impressed by Vane's ability, tries in his Memoirs to minimise his agreement with the heretical English revolutionaries; but he was in regular correspondence with them at least as late as 1653.

More significant was the link with the rebel Huguenot towns of Bordeaux and La Rochelle. In October 1651 the English Council of States was seriously discussing the despatch of an expeditionary force to La Rochelle, at the request of the town. There were long negotiations about sending English troops "to reduce France to the state in which England now is," as a hostile witness put it: to help to win for France "the precious liberty" which the Commonwealth had established in England was the way the Frondeurs' representative expressed it to Parliament. In 1651 the ex-Agitator Colonel Sexby and four others were sent by the Council of State to Bordeaux, where Sexby got in touch with the radical wing among the rebels. He translated the Leveller *Agreement of the People* into French, and offered it as the basis of a republican constitution for France, together with a declaration demanding protection of the poor against the rich. Sexby remained in France for two years. In May 1653 delegates from Bordeaux were sent to London, and as long as the Barebones Parliament remained in session it seemed possible that an English army would be sent to Guienne.

A propos of the appeal from Bordeaux John Rogers, the Fifth Monarchist, stated: "We are bound by the law of God to help our neighbours as well as ourselves, and so to aid the subjects of other princes that are either persecuted for true religion or oppressed under tyranny. What mean our governors to take no more notice of this? How durst our army be still now the work is to do abroad? Are there no Protestants in France and Germany even under persecution? And do not the subjects of France that lie under the iron yoke of tyranny send and seek and sue unto us for assistance? Well, woe be to us 'if we help not the Lord (*Judges* V.23) against the mighty'; for it is the Lord has sent for us thither, and calls for a part of our army at least into France or Holland. . . . As it is against the law of nature for the King of France to be worse than an enemy to his own citizens and subjects, so it is as much against the law of God, should they supplicate us for assistance, to be worse than neighbours. . . ." Clearly such a revolutionary sense of international obligations was being criticized by 1653; for Rogers continues: "Let not men dispute so much whether it be lawful to defend or strike in for another's liberty, if it were lawful to do so for our own, seeing we must love our neighbour as ourselves. If we love Christ in our own nation, why not in another?"

Between England and the Netherlands relations had been closer. The Dutch revolt had received enthusiastic support from Puritans and bourgeoisie, and the Dutch Republic was a model for them in the 17th century. The Dutch fleet had helped to prevent Charles I bringing over foreign military aid during the civil war. The Netherlands was the only country in which some approval was expressed of the execution of Charles I. In 1650 the House of Orange—closely related by marriage to the Stuarts—fell from power, and the States-General at once recognized the English republic. Negotiations began between the two powers for a close alliance or even a union, on the lines of the union of England and Scotland agreed on in 1652. But the economic interests of the bourgeoisie proved stronger than ideology. For the Dutch, the rulers of England were good protestants and good republicans: but they were also trade rivals, and the projected union was seen in Holland as a cool suggestion that English merchants should have free access to the Dutch colonial empire. Negotiations broke down, the English Parliament passed the Navigation Act aimed against the Dutch carrying trade, and war ensued.

But there were strong parties in both countries who opposed the war. If the English "could knock out Holland with one arm," said an English official, "political expediency must prompt them to raise her with the other, for the honour and glory of republics in general." Once it was shown that the English fleet could not be defeated, the Dutch government was prepared to accept the Navigation Act; when Cromwell became Lord Protector he soon put an end to the war. "It ought to be our principal aim," he told Dutch representatives in November 1653, "to obtain security against [the] house of Austria, and to organize our affairs in such a way that we did not need to fear anybody's power, and that we could dictate the law concerning commerce to the whole world." The mutual interests of the two republics were shown by an agreement that the Dutch should expel the exiled Stuarts from their territories and that the House of Orange should be excluded from office in Holland.

VI

As the English bourgeoisie began to consolidate themselves in power, the ruling groups became less and less influenced by ideological considerations, more and more by economic interests. As the Dutch war had shown, they thought less of international protestantism, more of the commercial and political interests of England. Popular hatred for catholicism was diverted from a European crusade against the great reactionary powers Spain and Austria into a colonial war for the subjugation and exploitation of Ireland. Some Levellers, to their credit, saw through this misuse of religious slogans. Walwyn was reported to have said "the cause of the Irish natives in seeking their just freedoms was the very same with our cause here in endeavouring our own rescue and freedom from the power of oppressors." An anonymous pamphlet published in 1649 attacked in the same sentence the way in which "the Frenchmen dealt with the Waldenses" and "the English hunted the poor Irish." When war was finally declared on Spain, it was in alliance with Catholic France, and its object was to grab colonies.

Cromwell was reported as saying that under Charles I "England had ruined the protestant party in France"; and now "England must restore it." Clearly Oliver was thinking primarily of the interests of the nation which he now ruled, not of the revolutionary cause as such. This attitude became dominant after 1653. The "protestant interest" became once more an asset of English foreign policy. It was important, for instance, to persuade the Swiss protestant cantons that England would protect their interests against the Hapsburgs better than France. They were offered English subsidies and support only when they were actually engaged in war and in so far as they accepted English guidance. It was good for English prestige to have protestants from all parts of the world appealing to the Protector for help.

This was a purely nationalist policy. Its agents were no longer revolutionaries like Sexby, but worldlings with City connections like John Thurloe, and John Pell, Samuel Morland and George Downing—the latter both to be knighted by Charles II. Foreign protestants acted as vital sources of information for Thurloe's admirable intelligence service: similarly in negotiations for the re-admission of the Jews into England in 1655 their value as intelligence agents carried at least as much weight as the religious arguments put forward for their admission or the economic arguments against it.

Not, of course, that foreign protestants got nothing from the connection. English diplomatic intervention on their behalf, backed by a mighty army and navy, could considerably alleviate the position of persecuted minorities. The best-known case is that of the Vaudois. But here the contrast between the prophetic thunder of Milton's famous sonnet and the actual achievements of the English government on behalf of the victims of the massacre is significant. Money collected in England for the Vaudois was believed to have been embezzled; but the employment of Irish troops against the Vaudois was used to justify the brutal transplantation of the Irish to Connaught.

The "protestant crusade" ceased to be a real aspiration: it remained a legend, useful when appealing to the patriotism of royalist divines and presbyterian parliaments; useful too as an excuse for shipping disaffected radical troops to military service on the continent.

A man like George Fox, the Quaker, later an apostle of non-violence, felt that the revolution had been betrayed. In 1657 he wrote a letter addressed to the army leaders and the government, but intended "for the inferior officers and soldiers to read." In this he said: "Had you been faithful to the power of the Lord God which first carried you on, you had gone into the midst of Spain, into their land, to require the blood of the innocent that there had been shed, and commanded them to have offered up their Inquisition to you, and gone over them as the wind, and knocked at Rome's gates before now, and trampled deceit and tyrants under. . . . And if ever your soldiers and true officers come again into the power of God which hath been lost, never set up your standard until you come to Rome."

VII

Some of the revolutionaries spoke not only of the brotherhood of protestants, but also of the brotherhood of man. This goes back to Francis Bacon, whose conception of an industrial science which should be devoted to "the relief of man's estate" had a profound influence on many supporters of Parliament. But there were others. George Hakewill's spirited defence of the achievements of "the moderns" as against "the ancients" helped to inspire a belief in progress before 1640, and so in the possibility of the improvement of society *by man*. Hakewill saw that, thanks to the mariner's compass and transoceanic trade "the whole world" had been "made as it were one Commonweath, and the most distant nations, fellow citizens of the same body politic"; he described himself as "a citizen of the world." John Preston, leader of the Puritan party until his premature death in 1628, often expressed this in purely religious terms. Labouring to do good to mankind is godliness: "it is your actions that benefit men," not words. Against this background Milton's pronouncements on human brotherhood can be seen not as unique utterances but as the culmination of a long tradition: "Who knows not that there is a mutual bond of amity and brotherhood between man and man over all the world, neither is it the English sea that can sever us from that duty and relation."

By the radical groups among the revolutionaries this came to be accepted without question. Gerrard Winstanley, the Digger, wrote a pamphlet which was signed by himself and forty-four others "for and in the behalf of the poor oppressed people of England and the whole world." George Fox addressed one of his earliest pamphlets *To the World* and another *To all the Nations under the Whole Heavens*: his followers carried this out by undertaking world-wide missionary activity.

Mary Fisher, who in 1657 set out to convert the ruler of the Ottoman Empire, later married a man of whom her highest praise was that he "desired the good of all mankind."

VIII

Did this sense of brotherhood between man and man extend across the Atlantic and Pacific Oceans as well as across the English Channel? Here we run up against difficulties. Three centuries of history of the British Empire have made the world sceptical of professions of good will towards native peoples uttered by men engaged in dispossessing those peoples. Clearly an element of hypocritical self-interest was there from the first. When in 1613 English merchants complained that treaties and contracts between Dutch merchants and rulers of states in the East Indies were invalid because extorted by force, their complaint was justified; but we may suspect that the welfare of the people of the East Indies was not their primary concern. Similarly, since Spain was trying to maintain a monopoly hold over trade with southern and central America, it was to the interest of English merchants and sea-dogs to enlist Indian help in their attempts to break open that monopoly. One should therefore be suspicious of expressions of concern about Spanish oppression of the American Indians in the mouths of Sir Walter Raleigh or John Pym, treasurer of the Providence Island Company. Subjectively they may have been genuine. But when an opponent of slavery on Providence Island began to assist Negroes to escape, he was promptly rebuked by the Company. "Religion," he was told, "consists not so much in an outward conformity of actions as in truth of the inward parts."

Nevertheless, however dubious the motives of the propagandists, the propaganda against Spain had its effect. Kind-hearted Puritans with no investments in colonial enterprises were shocked to read in their geography books of "the unparalleled cruelty of the Spaniards, who have killed, burnt and hanged about 50 millions of natives since their first plantation there." In 1621 a well-known London preacher, John Everard, was imprisoned by the Council for a sermon against Spanish cruelties in the Indies. There was thus a good deal of history behind the remarkable *Manifesto* which Milton wrote for Cromwell's government in 1655 to justify the declaration of war against Spain. It is, I believe, the first state paper ever to make a public grievance of the maltreatment of extra-European peoples by a great power. The Protector's government, Milton declared, properly used its naval power "in avenging the blood . . . of the poor Indians, which . . . has been so unjustly, so cruelly, and so often shed by the hands of the Spaniards: since God has made of one blood all nations of men for to dwell on all the face of the earth. . . . All great and extraordinary wrongs due to particular persons ought to be considered as in a manner done to all the rest of the human race." Whatever we may think of the motives of the English government, with the blood of countless Irishmen still reeking on its hands, there is still great significance in having the principle of human brotherhood thus officially proclaimed as one which should guide the actions of all states. Milton and very many English supporters of the government undoubtedly took the principle seriously.

IX

A desire for the conversion of infidels to Christianity was another claim frequently advanced by English colonists of which we are to-day rightly suspicious. Too often it merely served as a cover for aggression, subjugation and extermination of extra-European peoples. It was apt to figure more prominently on company prospectuses in England than in the activities of the early colonists. And it had its economic point. When the Indians were converted, observed Hakluyt, Purchas, and many others, they would naturally wish to wear Christian garments, and that would be good for the English cloth trade.

But after the initial period of settlement there are cases in which individual Englishmen—usually religious or political radicals—showed a genuine concern for the welfare of such peoples. Roger Williams, for instance, contested the King of England's right to grant the colonists lands which belonged not to him, but to the Indians who hunted over them. He demanded that the Indians should at least receive compensation. Under his influence slavery was abolished in Rhode Island. The Quakers also have an excellent record of behaviour towards the American Indians, George Fox being one of the first Englishmen to declare publicly against slavery. John Eliot, "the Apostle to the Indians," preached to them in their own tongue and translated the Bible into the dialect of the Massachusetts Indians in 1658. A concern for the welfare of the "ignorant Nations of the Earth" was one of the lessons Richard Baxter had learnt by 1664, thanks to the activities of Eliot and the Society for the Propagation of the Gospel in New England. For the cynical it is worth recording that the treasurer of this Society, Baxter's friend Henry Ashurst, was a wealthy war profiteer and one of the principal traders to America. As early as 1649 at least one Englishman attacked merchants who pretended their object was to convert the heathen but in fact engaged "in robbing of the poor Indians of that which God and nature hath given them; . . . and although their dealing concerning the Indians' goods be bad, yet they deal worser with their persons; for they either kill them, which is bad, or make them slaves, which is worse: I know not what to say concerning such impious proceedings with them poor innocent people." The author goes on to link up exploitation at home with colonial oppression and war abroad: the rich oppress the poor, and use them to "rob the poor Indians" or to "kill our neighbour tyrant's slaves" when (because of some supposed injury) war is declared and we "send some of our slaves to kill some of their slaves, and then one innocent shall kill another."

After 1653 it was clear that no continental country was going to follow England's example. At home the big bourgeoisie in town and country slowly brought the radical revolutionary movement under control. Colonial adventures in Ireland and the West Indies, commercial wars against the Netherlands and Spain, all helped to divert the interests, dissipate the forces and betray the ideals of those who had believed that an international revolution was to usher in the brotherhood of man. The English revolution was a *bourgeois* revolution: one exploiting class succeeded another in political power. By the end of the sixteen-fifties the revolutionary groups had been broken up, or, deciding that God's kingdom was unattainable in this world, had relapsed into quietist and pacifist religions. It was 130 years before the common people of France, and longer before the common people of England were able to express their sentiments and aspirations as freely as had been done in England between 1640 and 1660. Nevertheless, during those two decades, words had been spoken and principles proclaimed which were never to be forgotten. Despite all the bourgeois hypocrisy which, then and since, has sullied the principles of internationalism and human equality, it is worth recalling when and by whom they were first enunciated as a programme possible of attainment on earth. "I believe," wrote a New England Puritan in 1647, "that the light which is now discovered in England . . . will never be wholly put out, though I suspect that contrary principles will prevail for a time." He proved right on both points.

EMERGENCE OF THE CONCEPT OF REVOLUTION *

Karl Griewank †

The word *revolution* entered the domain of political thought proper by way of natural philosophy [science]. The growing importance of the word for astronomy, and for science generally, coupled with an inclination to fit each change of the heavenly bodies into an astrological or scientific scheme, helped to make the word *revolution* an ever more popular term and paved the way for its introduction into the language of politics. Sixteenth- and seventeenth-century theorizers were very prone to link both the name and the course of every kind of cosmically-determined upheaval with that regular circulation of the firmaments to which Nicholas Copernicus had devoted his principal work, *De Revolutionibus Orbium Celestium* [*On the Revolutions of the Heavenly Bodies*]. People were taking it for granted that the world they lived in was full of change. They could detect change most readily in political affairs, but there was no mistaking it in religion, mores, institutions and inventions as well: after all, a change in religion was often the evident cause of political change. Scientists, political theorists, and statesmen alike came to occupy themselves with the question of how these changes, the decisive and sweeping political changes especially, were related to the motions of the heavens. So sober a thinker as Bodin did not disdain such endeavors [nor did the brilliant Johannes Kepler]. Kepler had, through observation and mathematics, discovered the laws of planetary motion, the foundation of celestial mechanics, which had hitherto been inaccessible to the purely speculative Aristotelian conceptions that had prevailed. Yet this same Kepler, for all that he fought against the

* The concept of revolution as forcible and fundamental political innovation was unknown to antiquity and the middle ages. Professor Griewank, who at the time of his death in 1953 was Dean of the Philosophical Faculty in the University of Jena (German Democratic Republic—East Germany), here traces the emergence of the modern concept of revolution in the sixteenth and seventeenth centuries.

† Karl Griewank, *Der Neuzeitliche Revolutionsbegriff* (Weimar: 1955), pp. 171–182. Translated by Heinz Lubasz with permission of the publishers, Hermann Böhlaus Nachfolger. With one exception, the footnotes have been omitted.

superstitious pseudo-prophecies of the astrologers, constantly tried to puzzle out in what way the fluctuations in the affairs of men were connected with the motions of stars and constellations, believing as he did that the creator had instilled the same geometry and harmony into all things, creatures possessed of a soul and heavenly bodies alike. This pioneer of the new physico-mathematical science sought gratification for his intellectual longings in a speculative system deriving from Platonic and Neo-Platonic ideas, a system in which earthly creatures and heavenly bodies were embraced in a single universal harmony and were also jointly subject to disturbances. He associated the appearance of comets with the genesis of "protracted evil doings" (*langwirige böse Händel*) which [according to him] were not to be attributed solely to the "departure of a potentate and the changes in government ensuing thereon" (*Abgang eines Potentatens ond darauff erfolgende Newerung im Regiment.*) To be sure, Kepler himself was on his guard against the attempts of the "great crowd of astrologers" (*grossen Haufen der Astrologen [vulgus astrologorum]*) to conclude from the "revolution" of an astronomical year to a *Revolutio Mundana* [earthly revolution], to a lawlike regularity [*Gesetzmässigkeit*] in earthly affairs during the same time-span. But the belief in a very precise correlation between celestial motions and worldly changes nevertheless took root far and wide. It found expression, for example, in a dictum attributed to Kepler's Italian contemporary, Galileo Galilei: "The revolutions of the globe we inhabit give rise to the mishaps and accidents of human existence."

This new picture of a universe of stars rotating in regular motion, and of the earth moving within it, gave many people something to hold onto in their attempts to understand life and the world at a time when they no longer found security in the medieval-Christian doctrine of a harmonious world order. The astronomical conception of *revolution* suggested that it was possible to fit worldly changes into an orderly scheme; and this thought provided one important impetus, though not the only one, for the introduction of this conception into the language of politics. This despite the fact that the traditional desire prevailed for a time to conceive of change as circular, as a return to the good old ways, and so to think of *revolution*—akin to the ancient idea of *reformation*—as a turning away from abuses, lapses, and aberrations. Bodin, for example, sought to interpret the "conversion" to monarchy of insecure democratic and aristocratic regimes as the *re*-establishment of a stable and felicitous state of affairs. When Henry IV (Bodin's ideal king) disarmed his enemies, the League, by converting to Catholicism, and they all one by one went over to his side, it was widely said, "This is a revolution"—meaning that a reversion to a state of affairs similar or equivalent to an earlier one had taken place as irresistibly as a star rotates, so that resistance to it had become pointless. The contemporary *Histoire des dernières troubles de France* of 1599 observed that the king had accomplished a salutary change in the state (*changement en l'Estat*) at a moment when sun and moon were propitiously placed.

The great English Revolution of the seventeenth century (a term which may be used to designate the whole course of development from the outbreak of the Great Rebellion in 1640 to the Glorious Revolution of 1688) has often been made the basis of a cyclical conception of revolutions, following Polybius' old cyclical theory of constitutions: from the collapse of monarchy and aristocracy through a more and more democratic republic to military dictatorship and eventually back to monarchy. A cycle of this sort did indeed recur in the great French Revolution, and one can find it adumbrated in classical antiquity, in the Greek city-states and in the Roman Republic. But this must not be allowed to obscure the fact that modern revolutions [do not simply return to their starting points; they] always have further effects which shape and direct the subsequent development of the nation, and of those nations connected with it. We must understand the English Revolution in terms of the same preconditions as the Dutch struggles for independence from Spain which began in the sixteenth century (and which, in their turn, strike us as so much more modern than the Swiss struggles of the fifteenth). The thrust of political revolution took several directions, which stemmed from a spectrum extending all the way from conservative Calvinism to the anti-ecclesiastical, chiliastic sectarian movements of religious Puritanism. These revolutionary assaults were directed against the royal, episcopal, established church; against the monarchy itself; against compulsory religious institutions; and, finally, against every sort of political discrimination against the less powerful. The common objective of these endeavors was to secure the personal rights of individuals—rights which were derived from the birthright of free Englishmen (a right supposedly dating from Saxon times, but not extended to Papists or unbelievers); from the divinely-ordained right to freedom of conscience; and from the natural right to life, liberty, and property—three kinds of right that largely merged into one another. Chiliastic movements—which, incidentally, were increasingly coming to accept the principle of private property—were defeated by socially more conservative movements like Cromwell's which aimed only to change the social and political situation of certain segments of society without altering the structure of society as a whole. Parliament, which was evolving from an assembly of estates into the acknowledged organ of popular representation, gained the ascendant over king and church. At the same time it accepted as the fundamental principle of the constitution, if not the explicitly democratic ideas of the Rebellion, then at least the inherent individual rights of all Christian Englishmen (Catholics excepted). These changes acted as powerful forces making for the integration of the English nation and of that growing number of nations in the old world and the new which followed its example.

It has been shown elsewhere, in conjunction with some striking texts,[1] that it was not the—to us—revolutionary events of the years 1640 to 1660, but rather the return to tranquil conditions and to the old order, which some people at the close of the "Great Rebellion" connected with the motions of the firmaments and welcomed as a *revolution*. In the House of Commons Clarendon introduced the restoration of the monarchy with the following words: "The good genius of this kingdom is become superior and hath mastered that malignity, and our good old stars govern us again." And Hobbes, the sworn enemy of all insurrection against a political authority [which he conceived of as having been] created by a contract of all the citizens—Hobbes writes at the close of his *Behemoth* concerning the acts of the Long Parliament, on the occasion of Charles II's return: "I have seen in this revolution a circular motion of the sovereign power through two usurpers, father and son, from the late king to his son." In fact, he was overjoyed to see that now, at the close of the upheaval, Parliament was definitively conceding to the king a right which hitherto he had only been able to derive unilaterally from his sovereign title. This it was that Hobbes regarded as the positive outcome of the whole matter. The republican Commonwealth of 1649 had, for its own part, sought to legitimate itself with the claim that it represented the restoration of ancient liberties. In that way it had made allowance for the still deep-seated desire for a return to the olden ways; the legend inscribed on the Great Seal of 1651 read: "In the third year of freedom by God's blessing restored." In just the same way Charles VIII of France, upon the overthrow of the Medici

[1] E. Rosenstock, "Revolution als politischer Begriff in der Neuzeit," *Festgabe der rechts- und staatswissenschaftlichen Fakultät in Breslau für Paul Heilborn,* Abhandlungen der Schlesischen Gesellschaft für väterländische Cultur, Geisteswissenschaftliche Reihe, 5. Heft (Breslau: 1931), pp. 83–124, at p. 90f.

in 1494, had had himself fêted as the restorer and protector of the freedom of Florence (*restitutor et protector libertatis fiorentinae*). In all these instances the concept of the cycle was employed for the purpose of justifying a new state of affairs which, following upon an upheaval, was looked upon as final.

But the concept of revolution which astronomy had made familiar did not remain restricted to such conservative usage in the quest for tranquillity and permanence and, thus, in a restorative sense. It would in fact be completely wrong to ascribe the introduction of the concept of revolution into politics and statecraft to astrological speculations and astronomical parallels exclusively, or even to regard these as having played a decisive and enduring role in the transmission of the concept. At a time when political thinking was becoming more flexible, the keen political mind could see a variety of possible applications for the simple notions of revolving, rotating [*Umwälzung, Umdrehung*]. In the seventeenth century the word *revolution* was already linked with that objective, non-evaluative conception of *transformation* introduced by Machiavelli on the basis of classical models, and subsequently extended to the social realm—albeit, once again in a more limited and conservative sense—by certain French statesmen. A new, dynamic conception of political change underlies the words which the Duke de Rohan used in dedicating his *Interest des Princes et Etats de la Chrestienté* to Richelieu in 1634, a conception of change that is no longer bounded by fixed conditions and that flies in the face of every known piece of political wisdom, ancient or medieval: "Whatever it is that causes the cyclical revolutions of the things of this world, also causes the basic principles of good government to change." Revolution here becomes synonymous with reversal and alteration in things political, and with alteration in the world generally. The word *revolution* replaces the old terms *mutazione, commutatio, conversion,* and *changement* to denote alterations that have taken or are taking place on the objective plane; and though it does not denote subjective manifestations such as insurrections and conspiracies, still it carries with it that overtone of restlessness and movement which attaches to it from earlier and vulgar usage. Therewith the word *revolution* becomes the standard term for the doctrine of political and worldly change whose emergence we have been able to trace from the sixteenth century on.

The most important step in the history of the term was the event which permanently introduced the word *revolution* into historical writing and political theory—the Glorious Revolution of 1688. In contrast to the period of the civil war (1640–1660), which had been introduced into historiography by its first historian, Clarendon, as "the Great Rebellion," the later event, which brought about lasting political changes with far less internal turmoil, was unequivocally labeled a *revolution*. Historically, that was in keeping with current usage. A history of *England's Revolutions from the Death of the Protector Oliver to the Restoration of the King* (Charles II) appeared in Paris in 1689. It was a very superficial chronicle, most deferential to monarchy in general and to the French monarchy in particular. The author takes it for granted that his readers will take transformations of the kind he describes to be *revolutions,* not in the modern sense, as being manifestations of insurrection and disintegration, but simply as being turbulent changes in the body politic. The undertaking which had led to yet one more revolution of this kind was termed *glorious* because of its successful outcome: writers of biographical and political apologias for William of Orange thought it important to call his domestic and foreign policy illustrious because it was successful. By calling it "the Glorious Revolution" they meant that it was really just one more change of sovereigns, albeit one that had taken place in circumstances reflecting glory on the king and on the nation represented in Parliament. An apologetic tract in Latin, published in London, correctly translated the phrase into the ancient wording: *"insignis nostra rerum commutatio"* or *"rerum conversio." "La dernière Révolution d'Angleterre"* [England's latest revolution]—with this phrase one more change was added to a long line of changes.

For all that, the Glorious Revolution constituted a new point of departure for the political significance of the concept of revolution. The application of the word *revolution* to this event may be regarded as a counterblow to the restorationist concept of revolution held by Clarendon and Hobbes: a victorious Parliament was snatching from the hands of a king who had jeopardized the laws of the land, from the hands of a king in flight, the very concept of revolution that had been used in behalf of his predecessor! In the same way the concept of restoration, which had first been used by rebels, in Florence and then in London, to signify a "restoration of liberty," had subsequently been turned against them and used in behalf of the restored monarch.

The Settlement of 1688–89 was not an act of reversal. It was the confirmation of a constitutional state of affairs which Parliament considered it essential to legitimize in accord with all extant principles of English law, historical and natural. It was, therefore, a revolution only in the sense that it was a return to stable conditions after a period of fluctuation. It was a "liberation" of the Church of England and of the English nation from the arbitrary will of the monarch, a revolution without rebels or rebellions. But it was at the same time an event of the kind hitherto known as a *mutation*: a transition to a new dynasty upon new conditions which, with whatever foundation in law, had been laid down by Parliament. As an historical event the Revolution of 1688 itself soon came to be looked upon as something final and unrepeatable and, thus, as something not to be drawn into precedent [*"etwas theoretisch nicht weiter Verwertbares"*]. At the end of the eighteenth century Hume and Burke were still speaking of *revolution* as a unique historical event—and what they had in mind was the event of 1688. The naming of the "Glorious Revolution" was the beginning of the successful career of the modern meaning of *revolution* as a non-evaluative term for great transformative events, first and foremost in the political realm, but also for natural cataclysms and intellectual changes.

The American Revolution, which created another new nation by severing the ties of external dependence, was later to build upon the intellectual arsenal of the English Revolution. But with the Declaration of Independence and the founding of the United States that arsenal was once again enlarged in characteristic fashion. The equality of all men, their inherent and inalienable rights, and the sovereign right of peoples to institute their own governments were now no longer derived from historical or divinely ordained rights but exclusively from the rational right of nature which had been elaborated in west European thought. The French Revolution, however, being a process of purely internal transformation, was to have a truly incalculable impact upon the moulding of old and new nations in Europe and throughout the world. Its impact proceeded from a number of enduring fundamental principles. These principles were not drawn from the peculiar right of a particular people, as they had been in England; they were formulated in comprehensible terms of universal validity.

THE WORLD REVOLUTION OF THE WEST: 1763–1801 *

R. R. Palmer †

In the streets of Paris, on the ninth of Thermidor of the Year Six (July 27, 1798), there took place a long and memorable procession. It was in celebration of Liberty Day, as the anniversary of the fall of Robespierre was then officially called. It began at nine o'clock in the morning at the Museum of Natural History. First came cavalry and a band. They were followed by professors and students from the Museum, marching beside triumphal cars that bore various minerals, exotic plants, and some crystals presented by the people of Valais in Switzerland. There were also a live bear from the zoo at Berne, lions from Africa, and two camels and two dromedaries sent by General Bonaparte from Egypt. After more soldiers, and more musicians, came delegates from the printers of Paris, librarians of the public libraries, and professors from the *Polytechnique* and the *Collège de France*. Prize pupils from the new *école centrale* carried manuscripts and rare books. Next appeared teachers and students of the arts, who were followed by Art itself—the treasures captured by victorious armies in Italy: paintings by Titian, Raphael, and Paul Veronese, sculpture in stupefying abundance, the Laocoön, the Dying

* The late eighteenth century was a period of revolution in many parts of western Europe and in North America—in what is now called "the West." The view that we should therefore speak, not of "the era of the French Revolution," but of an "age of democratic revolution," or of a "world revolution of the West," has been most ably argued and supported by Professor Jacques Godechot (University of Toulouse) and by Professor R. R. Palmer (formerly of Princeton University, now Dean at Washington University, St. Louis).

† Reprinted with permission from *Political Science Quarterly*, 69, no. 1 (March 1954), pp. 1–14. Professor Palmer's view pervades his illuminating study, *The Age of the Democratic Revolution*, 2 vols. (Princeton: 1959, 1964), and was concisely set forth in a talk, "Révolution française, occidentale ou Atlantique," published in *Bulletin de la Société d'histoire moderne*, série 12, **59**, Bulletin spécial (1960), pp. 2–7. Professor Godechot's quite similar views may be found in the same publication, pp. 7–10, "Révolution française ou révolution occidentale? La deuxième phase: 1789–1815." They inform his brief survey, *Les Révolutions (1770–1799)* (Paris: 1963), which has an invaluable bibliography.

Gladiator, the Discus Thrower, and the Apollo Belvedere, to name only the most famous. Most conspicuous of all were the ancient bronze horses from St. Mark's in Venice. They bore an inscription: "Transported from Corinth to Rome, from Rome to Constantinople, from Constantinople to Venice, from Venice to France. They rest at last upon free ground." Numerous other inscriptions, up and down the procession, explained the assembled wonders to onlookers. One was a quotation from Seneca: "To live ignorant is to be dead."

All this plunder, for such most of it literally was, was ceremoniously presented to the Minister of the Interior, who received it at the feet of a statue of liberty. The festivities ended with the ascension of a balloon, or "aerostat," carrying aloft more inscriptions, together with "attributes of liberty and the arts," and the tricolor of the Revolution.

The men in the French government who arranged this extraordinary spectacle obviously intended it to have a symbolic meaning. It may serve also as a symbol for us. It may remind us of certain paradoxes, or seeming paradoxes, of the French Revolution: the association of liberty with force, of enlightenment and education with propaganda and histrionics, of a sense of progress with a sense of conquest, of soldiers with professors, of a feeling of attachment to the Western tradition with one of angry repudiation of the historic past. And the bears, lions, camels, strange plants, and imported statuary may suggest also the idea of a World Revolution, of which many people in Paris, and in other countries, believed France to be the center.

In the summer of 1798 France was bordered by other revolutionary republics in Holland, Switzerland and Italy. Belgium and the Rhineland had been annexed, and unrest spread through Germany. Ireland was in rebellion, and in Great Britain the government of William Pitt, to use the word of various British historians, was resorting to terror. In Sweden, said the British Foreign Secretary, half the people were Jacobins. In the United States, in July 1798, the same fear of Jacobins, that is of democrats, produced the Alien and Sedition laws; nor were such fears allayed when the democrats won the next election. The president of the college at Princeton, shortly thereafter, shuddered at "those irreligious and demoralizing principles which are tearing the bands of society asunder." [1]

The idea that these events constituted a world revolution, that is, a revolution of the Western World, is a very old one, since it dates from

[1] From an unpublished letter from Samuel Stanhope Smith to Jedediah Morse in the Princeton University Library. References in the present article are confined to direct quotations and a few other points which seem to be not generally known.

the eighteenth century itself. Recently, both in this country and in Europe, historians have begun to revive it. I need only mention our own Louis Gottschalk, or Georges Lefebvre of the Sorbonne, who, rewriting in 1951 his book of 1930 on the French Revolution, completely recast it to show the supranational implications. It may be that we should try to develop some integrating or unifying conceptions for this whole revolutionary movement in Europe and America taken together. It is not enough to have a rough semi-Marxist idea of the "bourgeois revolution," or simply to place different countries side by side for comparison, or to speak vaguely of the "influence" of France or of America upon a world left otherwise undescribed.

Such a world revolution may be bounded, for convenience, by the dates 1763 and 1800 or 1801. At the hither end, we have a dramatic close in the election of Jefferson to the American presidency, and the personal triumph of Napoleon Bonaparte in Europe. The two events were not exactly alike, to be sure, but both were followed by a decline of political agitation. At the same time, with the Peace of Amiens and the Concordat both the British government and the papacy recognized the consequences of international revolutionary republicanism, at least tentatively and pending further developments.

There are good reasons for beginning about 1763. With the decade of the sixties some of the characteristics of the revolutionary era become apparent—the ideas and issues, the alignment of protagonists on both the domestic and the international fronts, the types of political activity, and methods of rebellion against government, with the virtual creation of a public opinion on political questions in many countries. In the realm of ideas, the years 1762 and 1763 see the publication of the main writings of Rousseau, and we have it from Daniel Mornet, the leading authority, that the *philosophe* movement had triumphed by 1770. In 1765 the French Assembly of the Clergy issued its first wholesale condemnation of the *philosophe* literature, which it said would undermine, if unchecked, all churches, states, and societies. The same years of the mid-sixties bring, in France, the quarrel of Louis XV's ministers with the more or less united *parlements* of the kingdom. The cry of "Wilkes and Liberty" is heard in England, and the Sugar Act and the Stamp Act arouse America. No one can read E. S. Morgan's new book, *The Stamp Act Crisis,* without sensing what was to come. He himself calls the American agitation of 1765 a revolution nipped in the bud. It anticipated what was soon to happen, in America and elsewhere, both in the ideas employed, that is, the appeal to historic or natural rights against a sovereign authority recognizing no direct dependence on the people, and in the practical tactics devised, that is, gatherings of the merchant and lawyer class into clubs and committees, and their exploiting of mob violence to obtain their ends. At the same time the close of the Seven Years' War marked the triumph of Great Britain and in particular of its Parliamentary governing class, the most brilliantly successful of all people under eighteenth-century conditions, and hence the least inclined to see conditions changed. The stage is already set for the solid British conservatism which was in time to be the main support of counter-revolution, and for that British superiority in wealth, and command of the sea, with the consequent anti-British feeling, which were to affect all international relations for many years.

The problem now is to suggest a few unifying themes, running through these years, and more or less common to an Atlantic civilization.

To begin with ideas. To imply that ideas "caused" the Revolution has long been the signal for controversy, carrying the implication of a conservative approach. Since the Revolution, and indeed before, as in the French Assembly of the Clergy of 1765, there have been warnings that the literature of the Enlightenment made people unruly and filled them with impractical ideas. This is probably true. It is not the whole truth, for the ideas in question were more than mere rebellious opinions. They derived from centuries of European thought, and they applied to the actual conditions of the day. The whole issue as between ideas and circumstances in the causation of the Revolution was set forth with extraordinary clarity, as early as 1799, by Friedrich Gentz.[2] In 1790 a French conservative, Sénac de Meilhan, in his book of that year, remarked that "the French Revolution seems to be a revolution of the human mind."[3]

The main idea, if we must single one out, seems to have been a demand for self-determination, a sense of autonomy of the personality, a refusal to accept norms laid down outside the self, leading sometimes to a profound subjectivity, or an insistence on self-expression rather than adjustment to preëxisting authoritative standards. This seems to be the

[2] Friedrich Gentz, *Historisches Journal* (1799), immediately translated and published by Mallet du Pan in his *Mercure Britannique* (London, 1799) which appeared also in English as the *British Mercury*. Both Gentz and Mallet du Pan were writing as journalists in the service of the counterrevolution. Gentz's analysis may be read in English in the *British Mercury* (April 30 and June 15, 1799).

[3] G. Sénac de Meilhan, *Des principes et des causes de la Révolution en France* (London, 1790), as quoted in a hitherto unpublished work on French counter-revolutionary thought by Professor Paul Beik.

message of Rousseau, in the *Confessions* and the novels as well as in the *Social Contract.* In the latter, it is a collective self that defines the right; and each citizen is triumphantly demonstrated to be subject and sovereign at the same time. The same note of personal autonomy underlies all the practical demands for liberty, political and economic. It may be found in Kant's metaphysics and in his political theory, and in the world-creating Ego of Fichte, who believed himself and his philosophy to be part and parcel of the revolutionary movement. It presumably explains what Hegel meant when he said that Mind became fully free only with the French Revolution. It inspired the educational doctrine of Pestalozzi, who welcomed the revolutionary Helvetic Republic in Switzerland. It has been found, by those versed in music, in the work of that obstreperous republican, Beethoven. It is obviously central to romanticism, and, in the demand for spontaneity and the rejection of artificial restraint, inspires the *Lyrical Ballads* of 1798. Surely there exists here the opportunity for what modern parlance knows as a "synthesis," bringing together not only many peoples of different language or nationality, but also many different fields of activity and thought.

It might be shown also, in such a synthesis, how the universal impulse to liberty is at least in principle kept in order. Anarchic individualism is avoided, in the political sphere, by the stress on the equality of rights, and by the ideas of fraternity and of law; and all are bound together in the idea of constitutionalism. About fifteen new written constitutions were proclaimed in America, and ten in Europe, in the quarter-century ending in 1801. In economic theory, it is natural law, or the natural harmony, that prevents liberty from degenerating into confusion. In the arts, a generation that revived the sonnet can hardly be charged with looseness. In moral philosophy, with Rousseau and Kant, it is the human conscience that stands between freedom and anarchy. In more recent times, with the ideas of conscience and natural law losing their force, and the drive for emancipation or self-expression as strong as ever, a great deal of trouble has been attributed to such ideas. Some have sought philosophical composure in the Middle Ages. The matter cannot be amplified here. Suffice it to say that liberty has always been known to be dangerous.

A unified conception of world revolution would be the easier to arrive at if we could point to an organized and centrally directed revolutionary party, international in its operations. Conservatives in the 1790's, unable to believe that revolutionary sentiment had any real or, so to speak, legitimate foundation, naturally imagined that such an international conspiracy was at work. The French *émigré* Barruel, and the Scotsman John Robison, independently produced large treatises proving its existence. In this country Jedediah Morse spread the same alarm. There was, however, no such international organization. Agitators and subversives did exist in all countries, and sometimes French generals or civil commissioners in neighboring states employed secret agents. They had little or no connection with each other, or with the French government or any supersociety in France. The French Jacobins were never secret, and had no organization after 1794. Revolutionary secret societies were more the consequence than the cause of the great revolution of the 1790's. The Italian Carbonari, for example, may be traced to a kind of Jacobin club in Burgundy in 1790. It was in a Paris prison, in 1795, that Babeuf launched the revolutionary underground of the nineteenth century. In 1798, when all England was reading the shocking revelations of Barruel and Robison, the House of Commons appointed a Committee of Secrecy to inquire into subversion. The committee made the strongest possible case to show a conspiratorial movement in England since 1792. It published numerous documents, and it named names. No French agent is mentioned in its report, and no foreigner other than Irish.

Class analysis offers another common theme. Carl Becker once observed of the American Revolution that, with the question of home rule settled by independence, it remained to be seen who should rule at home. Thus the establishment of independence was followed by the heightened democratic agitation of the 1790's. The same pattern can easily be seen in parts of Europe, especially in regions subject to a sovereignty increasingly felt to be foreign. Cases in point are the Lombard and Belgian provinces, under the Hapsburg emperor; or the Swiss territory of Vaud, which belonged to the canton of Berne. In Belgium the assertion of independence in 1789 was followed by the strife between Statists, the upper class of the old régime, which wanted no internal change, and the democratic or "Vonckist" party, which demanded new rights for the hitherto unprivileged classes. The same pattern can be traced even in countries having native governments, since under the old régime all governments were in a sense foreign to their populations, the lack of moral bond between ruler and ruled being precisely the point at issue. It is now generally agreed that, in France, the revolution began with a revolt of the nobility against royal absolutism. This was no mere prelude, but an integral phase of the movement. If this revolutionary rôle of the aristocracy is once fixed in mind, then the attempts of Polish gentry to stage a revolution against the partitioning Powers, or the uprising of Hungary against Joseph II, can be brought into a unified conception of a general revolution. Even in England some of the gentry favored parliamentary reform; and parliamentary reform involving equal, individual, numerical, and "real" representation in the House of Commons, was rightly felt by conservatives to be a revolutionary change, both in the vicious practice and in the virtuous theory of the British Constitution.

In most countries having a middle class a bourgeois phase soon followed the aristocratic protest, and the sub-bourgeois or working classes were often heard from also, not only in France, but in England, Scotland, Holland and elsewhere. A historian of the city of Manchester, for example, remarks that the United Englishmen of 1797 offered the first example in that city of working-class political organization without middle-class leadership or support. In the long run, however, the landed interest seems to have had the last word, and it was the action of country people, perhaps more than anything else, that determined what happened as between one place and another. Only in France and America did small farmers become really revolutionary, and only in these countries do we find complete and thoroughly indigenous revolutions. In Ireland the rural population was disaffected, but helpless. In England the "land" meant a well-contented aristocracy. In Eastern Europe the very ownership of rural land was generally confined to nobles, who were the only political class, so that there was scarcely a tremor of revolution except for the noble opposition to outside Powers. In the Kingdom of Naples, the flimsiness of the so-called Parthenopean Republic of 1799 was due to the nonparticipation of peasants; and Cardinal Ruffo, with his famous Army of the Holy Faith, easily won back the country, not by the forces of clericalism, but because, being the administrative type of churchman, he had constructive ideas on land reform and could appeal to peasants.[4]

Class differences manifested themselves constitutionally, in almost every country affected by the revolution, in the question of whether the new state should be unitary or federal. In the Dutch provinces, the Swiss cantons, and the Italian republics, as in France after 1792, we hear the cry for a "republic one and indivisible." The same idea is evident in Belgium, in the German Rhineland and in Ireland with its United Irishmen, who believed that Irish Catholics and Presbyterians must combine indivisibly against the English. The idea of a republic

[4] This is the general thesis of N. Rodolico, *Il popolo agli inizi del Risorgimento nell' Italia meridionale, 1792–1801* (Florence: 1925).

"one and indivisible" was not primarily nationalist; at least, it had no necessary relation to linguistic or ethnic groups. It meant that persons struggling for a democratic revolution must integrate territorially for self-protection, since the old local units of province and town—Brittany and Languedoc, Bologna and Ferrara, Amsterdam and Rotterdam, Brabant and Flanders, Cologne and Mainz, not to mention the twenty-one boroughs of Cornwall—were everywhere the seats of entrenched, exclusive and self-perpetuating oligarchic or privileged families. To insist that these historically-developed corporate entities should retain a separate influence was called "federalism" in revolutionary parlance, and federalism was with reason regarded as one of the many aspects of counterrevolution. Advanced democrats everywhere demanded the dissolution of such entities into a uniform state built upon individual citizenship. It seems important to note that a contrary situation existed in America. The fact that Federalism in America meant the centralized state is a mere difference of words. The significant matter is that, in America, the advanced democrats continued to fear strong government, or any central government, and to put their trust in local authorities close to the people. In America it was the democrats who were "federalist" in the European sense. At a time when big government was even harder to keep under control than now, democracy in America was not committed to big government, as it had to be in Europe to exist at all. The difference is due, like so much else, to the fact that America had no old régime in the true European sense, and hence no such internecine struggle.

Finally, it is in the sphere of international relations, and especially in war, that a unifying conception for the era may be formed. It is the misfortune of our own generation to know something of the interaction between war and revolution, and we should perhaps therefore be able to analyze the corresponding phenomena of the eighteenth century with a dreary wisdom not given to Sorel or Von Sybel. Whether revolution must lead to war we cannot really be certain. It has been both affirmed and denied of the war of 1792. We do know that war can be a great breeder of revolution. We know, too, that war aims change during the stress of fighting; that governments or aroused peoples may crush enemies or seize and hold advantages in a way having little to do with initial ideology or intentions.

The revolutionary struggle, throughout the thirty-odd years, was inseparable from the struggle between England and France. The British government opposed every revolutionary effort—the American, the Irish, the Dutch of 1784, and the Belgian of 1789. It went to war with France in 1793 to maintain the *status quo* in Belgium and Holland, against which many Dutch and Belgians were in rebellion, but which for over a century had been favorable to British naval and mercantile interests. The French, on the other hand, under both the Bourbon and the ensuing republican governments, patronized virtually all revolutionary disturbances.

The French were the only people to make a lasting revolution by their own efforts. All others depended on them. The French shipped 30,000 muskets to America in the year 1777. Nine tenths of all the gunpowder used by Americans before the battle of Saratoga was from foreign sources, mainly French. It is clear that the success of the American revolt depended on France even before France openly intervened. In this respect the American Revolution resembles the revolutions twenty years later which produced the Batavian, Cisalpine, and other short-lived republics. The difference lies in the fact that the French withdrew from America, leaving the country independent, whereas they did not, could not, or would not withdraw from Holland or Italy except by abandoning their supporters to the counterrevolution.

The fact that the French alone accomplished a revolution with their own resources leads to comparative reflections on the Reign of Terror. There is no simple explanation for the Jacobin Terror of 1793. There is therefore no simple explanation for its absence. Yet the fact is that only in France did revolutionaries not depend on outside aid, and that only France had a real Terror. The Americans in the 1770's, and in the 1790's the Dutch and the Italians, managed to conduct revolutions of some magnitude without going to such lengths as the French in 1793. One reason surely is that they did not depend on their own precarious revolutionary resources–unorganized, unreliable, shifting, opportunistic, and virtually ungovernable, as resources of men and material in time of revolution are. They expected and received the aid of France. As a working hypothesis, we may suppose that revolutionaries had three alternatives: either capitulation to the old régime, or terroristic control of the means of defiance, or the acceptance of outside aid. The French did not have the third alternative. Of others, including our own esteemed Founding Fathers, it may be argued that receipt of French aid spared them the unpleasant necessity of terrorizing their fellow countrymen more than they in fact did. The matter is at least worth considering.

It is clear that war aims changed with war itself. The British government under Pitt, late in 1792, declared that it had no interest in the internal government of France, and would go to war only to preserve the existing situation in Belgium and Holland. Within two years, in July 1794, the same Pitt, in a secret cabinet memorandum, was planning to let Austria keep its acquisitions while Great Britain retained all those "already or yet to be conquered in the East and West Indies."[5] In five more years he doubted whether any lasting peace could be made except by restoring the French Bourbons—an opinion not shared by Prussia, Austria, or even the Bourbon monarchy of Spain.

The French went to war in 1792 in a spirit of crusading for liberty, of raising a world revolution against all kings and all nobles. As Brissot wrote, anticipating Lenin, "we cannot be at ease until all Europe is in flames."[6] As the Abbé Gregoire put it, in a phrase that would have suited either Metternich or Franklin Roosevelt: "If my neighbor keeps a nest of vipers I have the right to stamp it out, lest I be its victim."[7] But as early as 1793 a more national and hard-headed attitude began to prevail in France. There began to be a contemptuous feeling that no people except the French was really suited for liberty. The idea of world revolution gave way to the idea of revolution in one country first. Some writers, like Albert Mathiez, make a great deal of this change, which in a way relieved the Jacobins of responsibility for world turmoil. Actually the change made little practical difference. It is consequences, not intentions, that enter into the crude realm of fact. Since the enemies with whom they were at war were the privileged classes of Europe—the nobilities and town oligarchies and wealthy landowning clergy—the French republicans attacked them by attacking their sources of power, by abolishing their privileges, their laws, their tithes and their feudal rents, by summoning their former dependents to freedom, by granting equal rights to Jews, Protestants, Catholics, freethinkers, or whoever it might be that was outside the locally established church—and even by the confiscation of property, the property of hostile ruling classes, be it understood. Such procedure horrified conservatives, especially in England, where it was ascribed to some peculiar perversity in the Jacobin character, or to an excessive belief in abstract ideas. It was not altogether different from what happened to the South during and after our Civil War, or from what governments in general seem historically to have done in pursuing conquest or suppressing opposition. One thinks of the

[5] Great Britain, Historical Manuscripts Commission, *The Manuscripts of J. B. Fortescue Preserved at Dropmore* (London, 1892–1927), vol. II, p. 599.

[6] J. P. Brissot, *Correspondance* (Paris, 1912), p. 313.

[7] *Moniteur, réimpression,* vol. XIV, p. 587, session of November 27, 1792.

Celtic regions of the British Isles, and the Scottish Highlands as recently as 1745.

The point is that revolution does not have to be caused by revolutionary ideas. It may only be a weapon of war. The distinction is never clear. In France, even under the consulate and empire, there were many who remained attached to revolutionary ideas. They believed in principle in liberating men from feudalism, clericalism, or stupidity. Outside of France there were idealistic persons who first welcomed the French, then turned against them, disillusioned. The fact that they turned anti-French does not mean that in all cases they turned against revolutionary ideas, since the revolution was not French alone. They became the spiritual or actual fathers of the European revolutionaries of 1830 or 1840. The case of Michael Venedey is an example. He was a German republican of 1797, his son was a German republican of 1848.

Or again, if we say that revolution need not be caused by revolutionary ideology, we may have in mind that societies collapse for negative reasons, not so much from the strength of revolutionary sentiment as from the absence of any powerful sentiment in favor of the existing order. There were important revolutionary elements in Holland, Belgium, the Rhineland, Switzerland and Italy; but what caused the collapse of old governments and governing classes, in every one of these countries, was the war. More specifically, it was that they would not or could not defend themselves, that their own peoples did not believe in them, that there was no loyalty, faith or conviction on which to build, that they all were permeated by neutralism, and hoped plaintively, and vaguely, to be rescued by British money or the British fleet. In Holland in 1794 the Prince of Orange attempted a levy in mass; he is said to have raised fifty men. In Belgium the authorities were afraid to arm the people. In Italy it had long been unheard of for Italians to be soldiers. The Swiss had not fought in their own cause for generations. All fell before revolutionary republicanism, French and domestic.

The French, being at war, accepted assistance wherever offered. They stirred up the very dregs of society, as we may read in a hundred contemporary accusations. They brought the "masses," or at least a great many lower-middle-class and working people, into the practical politics of the Western World. By a historical irony, the liberal bourgeois awakened his Marxist doom. As for the British, being also at war, they brought into the practical politics of the Western World, though it would be premature to call it a Marxist doom, the mammoth power of Imperial Russia. No doubt historical irony can be overdone. Yet as early as 1775 there was talk in England of using Russian mercenaries in America. The Earl of Suffolk jocosely remarked that 20,000 Russians would be "charming visitors to New York and would civilize that part of America." [8] Vergennes, alarmed, foresaw that Britain might some day hire Russian troops for operations in Western Europe. In 1796 the British Cabinet agreed to give the island of Corsica to Russia. In 1798 Henry Dundas advised his cabinet colleague, Pitt, to "subsidize an army of Russians for British purposes," to attack Holland, defend Switzerland, capture Malta, open the markets of South America, or occupy Brest.[9] In 1799 there was talk of using Russians in Ireland. In that same year Vergennes' fears were realized when Russian troops, paid for by Great Britain, invaded Switzerland and Holland, on their way to France. It seems strangely modern to find Reubell, the former Director, declaring in 1801 that his policy of revolutionizing Switzerland in 1798 had prevented the Cossacks from riding into Paris.

The age of the French Revolution, it may be said in closing, has been used historically for a great many purposes. It has been used to explain the rise of nationalism or of liberalism, of class struggle or the "perpetual revolution" of Trotsky, to celebrate the freedom of thought, or, contrariwise, to demonstrate that dogmatic Jacobin ideology must lead to totalitarianism. Let us avail ourselves of the privilege of our predecessors, and use the revolutionary era to investigate what is most in our minds, to find out what a world is like that is divided by revolution and war. There is something to be said for leaving the national histories of France, or Italy, or Holland, to persons born or living in those countries. Perhaps we in America are best equipped to be the synthesizers. As that notable revolutionary, Thomas Paine, remarked in a notable revolutionary year, 1776, America is "the colony of all Europe." We are of all European nationalities, and of none; and so should be the better able to see the whole movement as one common to the Atlantic world. If we do, we shall not be mere innovators, nor be forcing the past to fit the present. We shall be saying what contemporaries before 1800 all but universally believed. We shall be performing the oldest and humblest of all the rôles assigned to history—the preservation of memory. Indeed, I am reminded of the very first words of the

[8] Keith Feiling, *The Second Tory Party* (London: 1938), p. 129. See also the *Parliamentary History*, vol. XIX (1778), p. 1355, where the use of 50,000 Russian troops is mentioned.

[9] The "Dropmore" or "Fortescue" papers, cited above, vol. IV, pp. 434–435.

first book of Herodotus, where he says that the aim of his "researches," as he calls them, is that the memory of the past may not be blotted out by time, that the actions of Greeks and barbarians may be known, "and especially that the causes may be remembered for which they waged war with each other." Each can decide for himself which were the Greeks, and which the barbarians. Or he may think that it was really a civil war in Hellas.

THE FRENCH REVOLUTION IN THE CONTEXT OF WORLD HISTORY *

Georges Lefebvre †

On the eve of the French Revolution, almost all of Europe was governed by what we now call the *ancien régime*. The prince enjoyed absolute power. The Church looked upon him as God's viceroy and in return he upheld the Church's authority by imposing his religion on his subjects. He had cast aside the concept of natural law, originating with the Stoics and developed during the Middle Ages by theologians like Thomas Aquinas, which assumed a society founded on free contract between governor and governed. Indeed, power had then been conceived only in terms of community welfare and was justified as a guarantee of the inviolable and legitimate rights of the individual.

To achieve absolute power, the prince had undermined seignorial authority and the political authority of the clergy, though allowing

* Professor Lefebvre (1874–1959), doubtless the most eminent student of the French Revolution since the death of Albert Mathiez, places the French Revolution squarely in its "Western" setting. But he also points out, *inter alia,* that the American Revolution was a very different affair from the French, and had more in common with the English Revolutions of the seventeenth century than with the French Revolution of the eighteenth.

† Georges Lefebvre, "The French Revolution in the Context of World History," in Peter Amann, ed., *The Eighteenth-Century Revolution* (Boston: 1963), pp. 83–91. Reprinted by permission of the publisher, D. C. Heath and Company. Professor Lefebvre's understanding of the French Revolution is presented more fully in *La Révolution Française,* 3rd edition, Paris, 1963. An English translation of the second edition (Paris: 1951) is now available: *The French Revolution,* 2 volumes (New York: 1962, 1965).

them to retain their social preeminence. In becoming subjects, the nobility and the clergy kept their privileges; the king, himself anointed and first gentleman of his realm, did not intend to submerge these orders in the masses. The Old Regime was indeed aristocratic in its structure.

There was a third feature characteristic of France and some other states. In these countries, while the prince had created a territorial and administrative framework, he had not carried this process to its logical conclusion. National unification was therefore incomplete, not only because of the diversity of legal systems, weights and measures, and the customs barriers which impeded the emergence of a national market, but also because the prince had granted or yielded special privileges to provinces and cities. In addition, he granted similar advantages to groupings, usually organized along professional lines, such as the nobility and clergy, so that society was hierarchical and partly "corporative." These estates implied privilege and therefore inequality. Absolutism, relying on "divide and rule," personified inequality . . . and besides, each estate, united by privilege and jealous of its superiority, demanded submission from those lower in the social scale. Nonetheless, the nation, created by submission to a single leader, by ties of material progress, language, and culture, remained divided territorially and socially. Even so, the French were better off than other nations: elsewhere the state, viewed as the personal property of the prince, took no account of national minorities, many of which were scattered among rival or enemy powers.

This regime faced two internal problems that were both political and social. The aristocracy (in other words, the nobility, since the clergy lacked social unity) resented the political impotence to which it had been reduced by the monarch whose power it dreamed of sharing. The nobleman, himself occasionally a victim of despotism, yearned for a freedom consonant with his dignity. This problem was a legacy from the past.

The other problem looked to the future. Ever since the tenth century there had developed a new class based on commerce, industry, finance, on personal rather than on landed property. This new bourgeois class had emerged from the Third Estate in a society in which land, as sole instrument of production, had entitled its owner to seignorial authority over those who farmed for a living. The king had drawn on these bourgeois both for money and officials, and they came to enjoy not only wealth but education and culture as well. Since the Renaissance, moreover, the new rationalism, exemplified by recent empirical science, provided an intellectual orientation consonant with bourgeois interests. Capitalism, which in its beginning phase had enjoyed mercantilistic state patronage, spread beyond the bounds of commerce to industry. The introduction of machinery opened such unlimited horizons for the bourgeoisie that the profits enticed even aristocrats to join in the exploitation of the world.

The bourgeoisie sought to obtain some share of power and therefore was willing to ally itself with the aristocracy against the king, yet bourgeoisie and aristocracy also were in opposition to each other. For centuries the middle class had striven for nobility; though this objective had not been altogether abandoned, the aristocracy was becoming more exclusive at the very time that the middle class, greatly increased in numbers, could no longer hope for mass ennoblement. The bourgeois, therefore, went beyond the nobles' demand for power and freedom to claim the end of all privileges as well as equality before the law.

At the end of the eighteenth century, because of the unequal pace of economic development, these problems appeared in a different guise in the various parts of Europe. Central and eastern Europe, which had long been backward by west European standards, did not partake in the new maritime trade routes and the exploitation of the New World which the great discoveries of the fifteenth and sixteenth centuries had opened up. The gap between East and West thus tended to widen. In this eastern and central European area newly-formed large states had adopted mercantilist policies and relied on the bourgeoisie for economic development and political organization. These states practiced what has been called "enlightened despotism." The mercantile middle class was, however, small in numbers, and the Enlightenment had more substantial influence on government officials, professors, and writers. The prince also confronted a threatening aristocracy. In Poland this nobility had seized power, while in Sweden only the *coup d'état* of Gustavus III had prevented a similar eventuality. In Hungary and Belgium the aristocracy had fought Joseph II to a standstill. In Prussia and Russia the monarchy had compromised, the aristocracy trading obedience and submission to the ruler for a free hand in dealing with their peasants whose serfdom, as one moved east, approached slavery.

In the countries of the south, particularly in the Iberian peninsula, the Counter Reformation had impeded free intellectual development. While Italy had been bypassed by the great overseas discoveries, Spain, in any case poorly endowed by nature, had been ruined by war. The nobility was somnolent, while the bourgeoisie grew only slowly. The peasant, as in France, did enjoy royal protection.

The maritime nations, Holland, England and a newcomer, the United States, offered a striking contrast to these land-based states. All of the former were Protestant. Holland and England had been the greatest beneficiaries of the rise of the European economy since the sixteenth century. In Holland the bourgeoisie was in control of the republic despite the nobility's support of the monarchist ambitions of the House of Orange. Since in this struggle neither constitutionalism nor liberty was at stake, it may be argued that a compromise between these three forces had either been reached already or was at least within sight.

While Holland had long been regarded as enjoying the greatest degree of freedom, the fame of the English and American revolutions, Britain's power and brilliant intellectual contribution made the Anglo-Saxon countries favorite antitheses to the absolutist regimes.

In England an aristocracy that enjoyed few privileges and no exemption from taxes differed markedly from its counterpart on the continent. Above all, only the lords formed a distinct legal estate, yet even their prerogatives were passed on to their eldest sons only. The younger children were commoners on a level with the gentry and squires who were represented in the House of Commons. The lords themselves could scarcely trace their genealogy beyond the Tudor era, since the nobility had been decimated by the massacres of the Wars of the Roses; hence they were not far removed from their middle class origins. Above all, however, since England was an island, the military character of the nobility had become attenuated or had disappeared altogether, to the point where military service was merely a matter of personal inclination. Consequently nothing stood in the way of the nobleman, even of the peer, going into business, and the distinction between the upper middle class and nobility was only a matter of ancestry and the kind of prestigious distinctions which were even within reach of the bourgeoisie. Nowhere else was there such social mobility: money alone defined class lines. The maritime and colonial expansion had consolidated a community of interest between the aristocracy and the capitalist middle classes. The Reformation, by sanctifying the struggle for naval and world supremacy waged against Spain and France, had heightened this solidarity. After the Catholic and Francophile Stuarts had, in the course of the seventeenth century, succeeded in rousing the whole nation against themselves, two revolutions had insured the final defeat of royal despotism. Yet neither the aristocracy nor the upper middle classes had directed their alliance against the monarchy as such. The Revolution of 1688 was a compromise establishing constitutional government which balanced king, lords, and a combination of gentry and middle class in the House of Commons. The latter was elected by a limited franchise which by its very lack of system insured the absolute control of the wealthy.

History was a source of precedents to be used against royal despotism. More than once the aristocracy had succeeded in extracting concessions from a monarchy that had appeared all-powerful since the Norman conquest, the most famous of these concessions being Magna Carta. English liberties were founded on such precedents and customs, in short, on tradition rather than on philosophical speculation. Even so, natural law had not been forgotten. It inspired Locke's justification of the Revolution of 1688. The importance of his works, which served as bible of all the continental *philosophes* of the eighteenth century, can hardly be exaggerated. However, once the Whig oligarchy had gained power, it gradually abandoned Locke as its intellectual mentor, since the contract theory, the recourse to natural right, could also justify democratic movements which loomed on the horizon threatening its power. On the eve of the French Revolution, Burke agreed with George III in considering the British constitution to be the most perfect imaginable. For Burke the constitution recognized not the rights of man but the rights of Englishmen: only the English had been able to conquer these liberties and they alone had clear title to them.

Not only did English liberty make no claim to universality, but the English state itself did not grant complete freedom of thought. Even though, like Holland, England enjoyed broader toleration than Catholic countries, the state religion was maintained. More important, equality before the law had never become a fighting issue. Because the aristocracy was allied with wealth, the upper middle class had never had to appeal to this equality. Political freedom had never undermined a determination to maintain the existing social hierarchy.

Anglo-Saxon America did not have to become quite so empirically minded. Natural right remained a vital force in these Puritan communities that had left Europe to escape, not only religious intolerance, but the weight of despotism and of aristocratic society. In breaking with the home country, the colonists appealed to natural right to justify their secession, while their declarations proclaimed the rights of man, not merely the rights of Americans. Their public law reflected this universality of natural law. At the same time the Protestant sects sought to safeguard their independence by insisting on religious liberty. There were, however, notable limitations: no one claimed any rights for colored men, and slaves remained slaves. Freedom of thought was not the rule and even though state and church were separated, it was taken for granted that religious liberty was confined to Christians. As in England, there was no insistence on equality. As the United States had never had peers or privileged persons the issue of privilege had never divided gentlemen and rich bourgeoisie. There were gentlemen descended from the British gentry who, living as noblemen on their plantations in Virginia and other Southern colonies, ruled over their enslaved blacks. Among these were the men who, like Washington, led the War of Independence and governed the republic during the first decades of its existence. However, men of a very different social background, such as Jefferson, had also become planters. Nothing prevented a Benjamin Franklin, printer turned merchant and journalist, from taking his place on the outer fringe of the ruling elite. Equality before the law for all whites, irrelevant as an issue in the struggle against Great Britain, had thus never been raised, nor was it ever considered a challenge to a social hierarchy based on wealth. Actually this equality before the law did not extend to politics, since the state constitutions restricted the franchise. What was called "democracy" in France during the first months of the Revolution was a government belonging not to the ruler or the aristocracy but to the nation. The actual procedures allowed, however, for the dominance of the moneyed class.

The English and American examples exercised a profound influence as the birthplaces of freedom. America, moreover, had stressed the universal validity of natural right. In practice this equality of rights, however admitted in principle, was not wholly applied, and in any case was not the basis for these revolutions. It is understandable that the example of these countries should have swayed not only the middle classes but also the continental aristocracy opposing royal power. For both, liberty seemed the pertinent catchword. Since equality had not been one of the consequences of these revolutions, it did not occur to the continental aristocracy, that liberty might endanger its social predominance.

The Anglo-Saxon revolutions had been directed against absolutism in behalf of a bourgeois-aristocratic alliance. The French Revolution was to be a very different affair.

From the socioeconomic as well as the geographical point of view our country occupied an intermediate position in Europe. Just as in other continental states, intermittent warfare had helped the nobility to preserve its military character. The very fact that this nobility faced impoverishment only increased its exclusiveness and its tendency to become a closed caste. Yet as a maritime nation France had also participated in European colonial expansion: its commerce was second only to that of Great Britain, while its industrial capitalism, though backward in comparison to the latter, nonetheless enjoyed the most advanced development on the continent. The French bourgeoisie, though closer to the land than the English middle class, was infinitely larger and more influential than that of any other continental monarchy. Perhaps most peculiar to French society was the important role played by saleable offices. The king had tapped middle class wealth by putting many official positions on the auction block. In order to increase their saleability or to gain the support of the officeholders, the king had endowed some of these positions not only with corporate privileges but even with personal or hereditary nobility. Just as in England, the infiltration of bourgeois families meant a renewal of the aristocracy. By the eighteenth century few nobles could produce a genealogy going back to the Crusades. This new nobility of the robe was establishing an increasingly intimate relationship to the military nobility. Nonetheless the nobility of the robe was not only businesslike in the management of its own affairs, but also kept up contact with other officeholders who had not graduated to the nobility. It also maintained ties with a socially less prestigious group, namely the lawyers. An intermediate class had thus developed which included these nobles at the top with officeholders in the middle, and commoners at the bottom. As a result of common professional outlook it shared the concept of law, of a legal order, of a monarchy whose prerogatives were limited by the sovereign courts' privilege of registration and remonstrance. Within this class a quite Cartesian rationalism and a tradition of the monarchy governing in cooperation with the wellborn and the well-to-do found special favor. Locke's ideas of natural right had fallen on fertile ground. In this respect, too, France occupied an intermediate position. While the absolute monarchy did cooperate with the Church in thought control, in contrast to Spain, Italy and Belgium, the Counter Reformation had not succeeded in stifling the development of philosophy and scientific inquiry. Finally, the French king had not had to yield power to the nobles; unlike England where a dominant aristocracy had uprooted the peasantry by enforcing enclosure, the majority of France's peasants were for all practical purposes free landowners.

Down to the time of the Fronde, the French nobility had often countered royal power with armed resistance. Even at that time the judicial officeholders had shown that they too could resist the monarch's authority. This reappeared once the hiatus imposed by Louis XIV was over, although its nature had altered as society had evolved. By the eighteenth century, armed outbreaks had become obsolete: the sovereign courts relied instead on a bourgeois appeal to public opinion, to constitutional tradition, to natural right. At the same time the aristocratically-dominated provincial estates played an increasingly important administrative role, particularly in Languedoc and Brittany. The office of *intendant* was preempted by nobles, as were the bishoprics. Commoners, already excluded from the sovereign courts in 1781 were barred from becoming professional officers, though they could still be promoted from the ranks. Aristocratic theorists, among whom Boulainvilliers and Montesquieu stood out, justified seignorial power by claiming that the aristocracy was descended from the Germanic conquerors of Gaul. Peasants complained over what historians have called the "feudal reaction," namely the increasingly exacting collection of manorial dues. It is clear, in any case, that some great landed proprietors benefited from royal ordinances permitting them to enclose land and to divide the commons. It is customary to concentrate on the eighteenth century growth of the bourgeoisie and the rise of the Enlightenment which reflected its aspirations. This period, however, was equally notable for the growing influence of the aristocracy, who attacked royal authority and successfully resisted all reform attempts that would have undermined their privileges, particularly exemption from taxation.

The French Revolution, in its first phase a revolution of the nobles, represented the climax of this rebirth of aristocratic opposition. By September 1788 when Louis XVI had been forced to call the Estates General, an aristocratic triumph seemed in sight. If, as anticipated, the Estates were to meet in three separate orders with the clergy dominated by the aristocratic episcopate, the nobility would be in control. This nobility was willing to help the king bring order out of financial chaos, but only at the price of certain concessions.

What were these concessions? The aristocrats demanded what they called liberty, that is, a constitutional government relying on regular meetings of an Estates General dominated by the nobility. In the provinces they would displace the *intendant*.

The nobility had no inkling that it was undermining the bulwark of its own privileges by weakening royal power. The nobility did not foresee that once the Estates had been called, the bourgeoisie would find its voice. Much as in England, the price of their cooperation was likely to be equality of rights. When this price was demanded the French nobility refused to make this concession. As a result the Estates General, intended as a battering ram against royal authority, saw the nobility thrown back on the defensive. A second phase of the Revolution had begun—the bourgeois revolution.

When Louis XVI accepted both freedom and constitutional government on June 23, 1789, some of the national objectives seemed to have been met. When, however, he threw his support to the nobility and clergy, this was tantamount to rejecting equality which henceforth became the crux of the struggle.

Actually the king, by means of his army, seemed capable of ending the conflict on his own terms. The artisans and peasants, however, whose own interest was unmistakable, supported the bourgeoisie. The popular and peasant revolutions, culminating in the night of August 4, broke the power both of the monarchy and the nobility. Unlike the bourgeoisie which had not aimed for the ruin of the aristocracy, the popular revolution wiped the slate clean and soon completed the social revolution by nationalizing church property.

In practice the consequences of this social revolution were not carried to their logical conclusion in 1789. A part of the manorial dues had to be redeemed; the Catholic clergy retained its monopoly of public religious services, its state financial support, its control of marriage, education, and welfare work. When the aristocracy and the monarchy looked abroad for support, civil war broke out. This civil war persuaded some of the midle classes to throw in their lot with the lower classes to complete the destruction of the aristocracy by confiscating the *émigrés'* property and by seeking to crush the clergy's influence. In these circumstances the revolution turned democratic: it adopted manhood suffrage, proclaimed a republic, freed the slaves, separated State from Church, and secularized education, welfare, and personal status.

This is the way in which the French Revolution gained its distinctive place in the history of the world. Although the revolution appealed to natural law (as the American Revolution had also done), its achievements left a universal imprint quite alien to British liberty. Its sheer momentum, moreover, was much greater. Not only did the revolution establish a republic but it insisted on manhood suffrage. Freedom for whites was not enough: the slaves were freed. Not content with toleration, the revolution admitted Protestants and Jews to full citizenship and, by secularizing personal status, recognized the individual's right not to belong to any religion.

All this, however, was secondary to the real mission of the revolution which was to be the revolution of equality. While in England and America the alliance of aristocracy and upper middle class had precluded a stress on civil equality, in France the bourgeoisie had been forced to emphasize it by the unbending attitude of the nobility. Indeed, by abolishing manorial rights, the peasants initiated equality with a vengeance. Since by revolutionary definition liberty was tantamount to obedience to lawful authority alone, liberty and equality were complementary in that liberty by itself would lead to privilege for the few.

In gaining freedom and equality, the French had become the Nation One and Indivisible. This new interpretation of national sovereignty is a third outstanding characteristic of the revolution from which grew France's claim that nations, like individuals, should be liberated. Thus France claimed Alsace, Avignon, and Corsica by appealing to free consent rather than to conventional treaties between rulers. International law was being revolutionized just as internal civil law had been. In this early phase the revolution looked forward to peace and cooperation among free nations united by the ideal of a society of nations, even of a universal Republic.

These characteristics explain the French Revolution's impact on the world and its long-range significance. At the same time, although these principles have since registered gains, it would be a mistake to attribute their dissemination solely to the revolution. The example of England and the United States had certainly not been forgotten. It would be equally false—and this is a widespread idea—to credit this ideological expansion solely to the magnetism of ideas: in areas adjoining France, the *ancien régime* fell victim mainly to the revolutionary armies led by Napoleon. Since that time capitalism has become the chief vehicle by which these new principles have conquered the world. These principles, as historians have sought to show during the last several decades, reflected the interests of the middle class who championed them. In granting economic freedom, abolishing serfdom, freeing the land from the burden of tithe and manorial dues, bringing church property back into the dynamic channels of the economy, the bourgeoisie was paving the way for capitalism. Wherever capitalism has penetrated —and thanks to its inner dynamic it has become ubiquitous—the same kinds of transformations have occurred. By strengthening or creating a middle class, capitalism has helped the triumph of liberty and civil equality as well as the development of nationalism, in our own day even among colonial peoples once dominated by the white man.

Nonetheless the French Revolution has retained an emotional drawing power unrelated to any selfish interest. It is associated with popular insurrection symbolized by the storming of the Bastille and the wars of liberation which the *Marseillaise* commemorates. This is the work of those who died for the revolution. To ignore the influence of class interests and economics on a movement of ideas would be a mutilated history. To forget that the bourgeoisie was convinced that its rise was identified with justice and the welfare of all mankind would be no less of a distortion. The fighters of July 14 and August 10, the soldiers of Valmy, Jemmapes and Fleurus risked their lives not from self-interest but because they enthusiastically embraced a universal cause.

Nonetheless this equality of rights, this essential principle of the French Revolution by which the bourgeoisie of 1789 rationalized the abolition of aristocratic privilege based on birth, had some unexpected consequences. The middle class, confident in its ability, power and prospect, had ignored the ill-tempered warnings of its opponents in this respect.

For this middle class, as for the Anglo-Saxons, equality meant equality of opportunity. Although everyone was free to take advantage of these opportunities, obviously not everyone had the requisite ability. What significance could freedom of the press or free access to public office have for someone who was illiterate? Yet public instruction was contingent upon being well-off if not actually wealthy. The bourgeoisie of 1789 interpreted the right to vote and to be elected in a similar spirit. This right, like others, required certain prerequisites, in this case the payment of a given amount of taxes as evidence of a certain standard of economic independence. Thus the rights of man and of the citizen, formulated by the bourgeoisie, were to remain largely academic and theoretical. There was little doubt, and none after Thermidor, that in the eyes of the middle class only property owners were entitled to actual, as against theoretical, power. Property being hereditary meant that privilege due to birth had not, as counterrevolutionaries observed, been eliminated after all. Democrats were soon to point out that private ownership of the means of production led to the subjection of the wage earners. Private property in workshops, the sole source of employment, made illusory the rights of the propertyless.

The lower classes, aware of these implications, had always opposed economic freedom which led to capitalism and the triumph of big business. Their ideal was a nation of peasant proprietors and independent artisans. In any case they sought state protection for the wage earner from the omnipotence of the rich. In order to gain power and organize the defense of the revolution after August 10, 1792, the republican bourgeoisie had accepted universal suffrage and continued its alliance with the so-called "sans-culottes." This alliance resulted in a compromise between the middle class aspirations of 1789 and the masses who called for government intervention to secure a more widespread distribution of property, public education for all, economic controls to keep prices and wages in balance, and a minimum social security system. This policy of "social democracy," initiated by the Mountain during the Year II, horrified and frightened the bourgeoisie and seemed to be banished forever after 9 Thermidor. When, however, republicanism reappeared after 1830, some of its followers took up Montagnard principles. With the re-establishment of universal suffrage in 1848, the application of these principles became one of the facts of political life.

Even during the revolutionary period, however, some groups had gone even farther by calling for the abolition of the private ownership of the means of production and the creation of a communist democracy intended to fulfill the promise of equality. This same intention has, in the final analysis, also made socialist theoreticians, particularly in France, present their systems as the completion of the French revolutionary achievements left unfinished by the middle classes. This is not to claim that the tradition of the French Revolution is the sole element in this development. Religious and humanitarian feelings have also been instrumental in aiding social progress. Above all, the transformation of the economy has had a powerful influence on the broad extension of equality of rights. The victories of capitalism led to trade union and political organization of the proletariat made possible by the concentration of business and labor, which defined and accelerated the class struggle. These organized elements could not be ignored. At the same time, the phenomenal productive growth engendered by capitalism, by increasing the resources available to human society, has brought a variety of welfare services, such as education and social security, within the realm of feasibility, whereas during and long after the revolution the cost of such services relegated them to Utopia.

Leaving aside differing approaches to history, the fundamental problem of our contemporary world appears to be the problem of equality within each nation and equality among nations. It is not the historian's job to prophesy how mankind will resolve such a problem; yet the historian can attest that the French Revolution not only raised this issue but also indicated various directions in which a solution might be sought. One may conclude, therefore, that, admired or loathed, the name of the French Revolution will long remain on men's lips.

THE REVOLUTION OF 1848 *

Henri Brunschwig †

The Revolution of 1848 was an international event and, apart from the world wars, the only such event in the West. But it did not affect all of Europe. At least two states—England and Russia, at opposite ends of the continent—remained unscathed. What made these two countries different from the others? The Revolution of 1848 shook those countries in which a bourgeois élite led the opposition against more or less reactionary governments. But Russia had no bourgeoisie and, after the electoral reform of 1832, the English bourgeoisie was no longer in opposition.

In the first place, then, the Revolution of 1848 was the act of bourgeois liberals. All over the continent, from 1815 to 1848, they sought to defend the privileges they had acquired under the French Revolution and the Empire against a reactionary nobility bent on re-

* By the very fact of their failure the revolutions of 1848 changed the course of history as decisively as they might have, had they succeeded. They had profound consequences for the future course of revolutionary movements in western and eastern Europe alike. In the following essay Professor Brunschwig, of the University of Paris, offers a somewhat unusual interpretation of their impact on France and Germany, respectively.

† Henri Brunschwig, "Propos sur la Révolution de 1848," *Annales,* 3 (1948), pp. 129–134. Translated by Melissa Nelken with permission of the editors. For further information on the several revolutions of 1848, the student is referred to a first-rate study, to which a useful bibliography is appended: Priscilla Robertson. *Revolutions of 1848* (Princeton: 1952).

covering its former position. These advantages did of course vary in importance from country to country. In France equality before the law was no longer an issue; the struggle now centered on property qualifications. Although large-scale industry did not yet exist, progress in production and exchange had been great enough to create a national market. Books and ideas traveled along with the merchandise and united the bourgeois and the artisans from one end of the country to the other.

In Prussia the reforms of Stein and Hardenberg were still to be completed. The abolition of serfdom and the agrarian reform were illusory in view of the continued existence of seigneurial jurisdiction and of an administrative system that, in practice, stopped the representatives of the central authority at the gates of the feudal domains. In Germany the bourgeoisie had long been dominant in the cultural sphere. The economy was traditionally under the direction of the government. But, once individual initiative was set free, the bourgeoisie asserted itself. Even the Prussian government, which kept the bourgeois from power and would hear nothing of a parliament, had to rely on them in order to carry out plans for the customs union. The barriers which divided Germany fell one after another. Social evolution—more rapid in one place, slower in another—followed a similar pattern in all the states.

I

The surge in population which had begun at the end of the eighteenth century continued everywhere. France's population increased from 27,000,000 in 1801 to 35,000,000 in 1846; Germany's, from 24,-800,000 in 1816 to 34,400,000 in 1845 (1914 boundaries). Cities proliferated: the 634,000 Parisians of 1816 became 1,360,000 by 1846. In Saxony and Silesia, where industry was concentrated, almost all of the cities at least doubled in population. Chemnitz grew from 10,000 to 50,000 people between 1816 and 1845. These populations, which were gradually reached by education, formed willing armies in the bourgeois cause. Such support from artisans and workers was only to be expected, since the reign of the bourgeoisie undoubtedly constituted, for everyone, an advance over the absolutism of divine-right monarchy. The bourgeoisie's goal was to establish constitutional governments, which would be more or less concerned with the fate of the masses of peasants and workers, who did not yet realize their own strength.

National feeling, which the wars of the French Revolution and the Empire had aroused, was also everywhere on the increase. The bourgeoisie was, by nature, less cosmopolitan than the nobility. It knew nothing of the blood ties which united the great aristocratic families; it substituted frontiers for the indefinite border zones which had existed between states in the days of feudal dependencies. Even its culture became more national in proportion as modern languages gained over Latin and as the hold of religion over public and family life diminished. In Italy and Germany national fervor found expression in the ideal of national unification. But the champions of unification were nonetheless liberals: they wanted a constitutional regime, if not a parliamentary one, on the model of the South German States, France, and England. For all bourgeois, habeas corpus and the rights of man were a political gospel to which they felt more attached than to any religious gospel. Moreover, liberal Catholicism proved to them that the two were not incompatible.

Between 1815 and 1848, then, population growth, commercial or industrial progress, urbanization, and national feeling developed along parallel lines in every European country. And everywhere this development reinforced liberal ideas. There is nothing puzzling in all this, since it seems clear that the formation of popular masses leads to democratization. What does seem strange is that the same demographic movement and the same accelerated economic progress did not continue to produce the same effects in the second half of the century. While the advance of democracy did continue in France and England, Germany became autocratic: 1848 was undoubtedly the closest the German people came to political liberalism in the nineteenth century. Thereafter they moved away from liberalism and took an opposite course to that of the western democracies.

We must, therefore, look for the international problem not in the revolutionary quake of 1848, but in its immediate consequences.

II

In France the Revolution of 1848 did not constitute a crisis in the special sense which we attach to this term: it did not upset a tradition, bury an ideal, or replace one way of thinking and feeling with another. The June Days crushed the Paris workers. The *coup d'état* of December 2 sent the republican bourgeois into exile. The police-state and military regime which Napoleon III established in 1852 was more authoritarian than were the regimes preceding the revolution. All this is indisputably true. But from 1857 on there were five bourgeois republicans in the legislature. The pre-1848 republican leaders, Thiers and Berryer, returned shortly thereafter. And in 1864 Ollivier was able, with the Emperor's consent, to form a third party, composed of bourgeois liberals who oriented the Empire towards parliamentary government. The workers, who were favored by a government which sought an ally in their leader, Tolain, aligned themselves with the opposition. The leaders of the republican party that they supported were lawyers, doctors, and bourgeois: until the end of the century the bourgeois continued to guide social and political development.

Always inspired by his illustrious model, Napoleon III did his utmost to establish a new aristocracy. But the bourgeois of the Second Empire were much less eager for titles than was M. Poirier.[1] We can measure the progress of liberalism by comparing the role played by the nobility during the First Empire with the unobtrusiveness of the primarily military nobility of the Second: it was no longer good form to be connected with the social classes of the past.

The greatest achievement of the Revolution of 1848 was to have emancipated the slaves and to have replaced mercantilist colonialism with a policy of assimilation which, mistaken though it may have been, was certainly generous. And though the Emperor did not allow representatives of the colonies to sit in the legislature and did return to the statutory system, whereby the chamber was excluded from colonial legislation, he had no thought of reinstituting the colonial pact. In Algeria he showed a real interest in the native population. And though more immediate concerns kept him from developing a consistent colonial policy, at least he did not interfere with people who had one: one cannot write about the Revolution of 1848, and especially about its international character, without recalling the political activities of Faidherbe in Guadeloupe and Sénégal. The care he took to educate the natives and to make them accept the French community made his work durable. Faidherbe's Sénégal was an achievement of the Revolution of 1848, and the ideal of the revolution was perpetuated there under the Empire, as it was in the Antilles and in Réunion. The Revolution of 1848, far from destroying a tradition, reinvigorated the ideals of 1789 in France.

In Germany it was a different story. The unindemnified abolition of hunting rights and seigneurial jurisdiction did endure in Prussia; but these were certainly the only lasting achievements of the revolution.

[1] A wealthy Parisian shopkeeper who marries his daughter to a poor nobleman in hopes of gaining social and political prestige; in *Le Genre de M. Poirier,* by Emile Augier and Jules Sandeau (1855). (Translator's note.)

The outstanding fact was rather the break with that liberal tradition which had asserted itself under Frederick II and Joseph II and had subsequently spread throughout the empire. The armies of reaction overcame the liberals in Germany more quickly than in France. Above all, they overcame them more completely. The bourgeois liberals, hunted down or simply too attached to their ideals to endure a regime of censorship and political police, emigrated en masse. On the eve of the revolution bad harvests led to a resurgence of emigration, which had long been driving peasants and artisans to seek their fortune in America. Ninety-five thousand left in 1846; in 1847, 110,000. The revolution, which aroused so many hopes, reduced the number of emigrants: it fluctuated between eighty and ninety thousand from 1848 to 1850. Then, in 1851, there were 113,000 emigrants; in 1852, 162,000; in 1853, 163,000; and in 1854, 300,000.

There was no economic reason for this rapid increase in emigration, which also involved the bourgeoisie. A large number of liberal leaders left the states in which the old regimes had been restored—Pastor Dulon of Bremen, Hadermann of Frankfurt, Karl Schurz. Teachers, lawyers, doctors, poets, musicians, and even officers left. Valentin estimates the number of those who emigrated between 1849 and 1854 at 1,100,000, perhaps 2½ per cent of the population. They took their fortunes with them, worth at least 300,000,000 thaler (900,000,000 gold marks). These were not poor men, but an élite whose absence was bound to make itself felt.

Not all of the liberals left, however; and their ideals of course continued to exist. Men continued to dream of unification, of a constitution, of socialism. But the meaning of these words changed, though the liberals themselves were not always aware of it.

III

To all appearances, in fact, the development of Germany after 1848 continued along the old lines. But unification by Bismarck, who created an autocratic empire, had nothing in common with the plans of 1848. It was an old-regime operation, a Prussian military conquest, not a communal venture like the federation of France in 1789.

The advance of democracy similarly appeared to be continuing, since social progress was being achieved perhaps more effectively than in the west. But French and English socialisms, long expounded by bourgeois liberals, continued to be pervaded by the ideas of 1789 and

1848. They remained humanistic until at least the time of Jaurès. In Germany the workers, for lack of a bourgeois élite, were organized more sharply along class lines and set their material demands above their humanitarian ideals. Marxism has always preferred economic equality to liberty. It is not profoundly democratic in the classical, bourgeois sense of the term.

In every case the same reality underlies the appearances: just as Bismarck achieved a unity different from the one dreamed of by his old adversaries, so he ended the Zollverein and subscribed to free trade, only to jettison it in 1878, as soon as he felt strong enough to satisfy the interests of his agrarian supporters; in the same way he promulgated, between 1883 and 1889, the accident, sickness, and old-age insurance laws which ameliorated the workers' material condition and made it possible to keep renewing, for twelve years (1878–1890), the laws excluding the Social Democratic party [from political activity].

The bourgeois who had not emigrated contented themselves with appearances. They did not understand the rare leaders who endeavored to enlighten them, the Jew Lasker or the Catholic Mallinckrodt. Moreover, they gradually became convinced of their own ineffectualness: was it not evident that their enemy Bismarck had succeeded where they had failed? Had not Bismarck, whom they had so long reviled, achieved unity, satisfied national fervor, and made socialism a reality? The liberal élite was seized by a sort of timidity: Bismarck must be right; politics was a profession, a technique. It was the business of the government, of the king and his ministers and generals, not of the professor, the doctor, or the weaver. Everyone should stay within the bounds of his own profession. Parties became coalitions of interests among which the government arbitrated. Their leaders did not prepare themselves for exercising power; and those who wanted to participate in public affairs climbed the ladder of the bureaucratic hierarchy or made their way into the class of nobles and officers which was closer to the seat of power.

A sharp split thus came into being between the opposition of 1848 and the new post-1870 bourgeoisie. This development was complete by about 1880: the German bourgeoisie was no longer liberal; its ways of thinking and feeling were the very antithesis of those that prevailed before the revolution.

And another split came about which was more enduring, more profound, and more fraught with consequences: a split between central Europe and the western nations. In the latter democratic development, after a momentary interruption, resumed under the leadership of the liberal bourgeois élites. In the former it came to a halt: a new, authoritarian tradition was created, dominated by the army, the nobility, and the bureaucracy, which culminated in the capitalist, Prussianized Germany of 1880.

The two blocs which trouble liberals today—whose formation they wish to prevent, whose boundaries they see passing from the Vistula to the Oder or from the Oder to the Elbe—these two blocs were formed in 1850, when the moral unity of the continent was shattered by the international revolution of 1848; and their boundary lies along the Rhine.

RUSSIA AND 1848 *

Isaiah Berlin †

The year 1848 is not usually considered a landmark in Russian history. The revolutions of that year, which seemed to Herzen like "a life-giving storm" on a sultry day, did not reach the Russian empire. The drastic changes of policy on the part of the imperial government after the suppression of the Decembrist rising in 1825 seemed all too effective: literary storms like the Chaadayev affair in 1835, the loose student talk for which Herzen and his friends were punished, even the fairly numerous but minor peasant disorders in the early forties mostly in remote provincial districts, were easily disposed of; in 1848 itself not a ripple disturbed the peace of the vast and still expanding empire. The gigantic strait-jacket of bureaucratic and military control which, if not devised, was reinforced and pulled tighter by Nicholas I, appeared despite frequent cases of stupidity or corruption to do its work. There was no sign of effective independent thought or action.

* There was no revolution in Russia in 1848. But the revolutions that took place elsewhere in Europe had a profound effect both on the Tsarist regime and on its opponents. The author of the following study is a Fellow of All Souls College and Chichele Professor of Social and Political Philosophy in the University of Oxford.

† Isaiah Berlin, "Russia and 1848," *Slavonic and East European Review*, 26 (1948), pp. 341–360, with emendations by Professor Berlin. Reprinted by permission of author and editors. A very full treatment of the history of Russian social, especially revolutionary, thought in the nineteenth century may be found in Franco Venturi, *Roots of Revolution* (Engl. translation), London, 1960.

Eighteen years earlier, in 1830, the news from Paris had put new life into Russian radicals; French utopian socialism wholly transformed Russian thought; the Polish rebellion of 1831 became the rallying point of democrats everywhere, like the Republic in the Spanish civil war a century later. But the rebellion was crushed, and all embers of the great conflagration, at any rate so far as open expression was concerned (the Galician rising of 1846 did not spread to Russian Poland), were by 1848 virtually stamped out—in St. Petersburg no less than in Warsaw. To observers in western Europe, sympathetic and hostile alike, the autocracy seemed unshakable. Nevertheless the year 1848 is a turning-point in the development of Russia as of Europe, not only because of the decisive part played in subsequent Russian history by revolutionary socialism, heralded by the Manifesto composed by Marx and Engels to celebrate its birth; but more immediately because of the effect which the failure of the European revolution was destined to have upon Russian public opinion, and in particular upon the Russian revolutionary movement. At the time, however, this could scarcely have been foreseen: well might a sober political observer—a Granovsky or Koshelev—feel gloomy about the possibility of even moderate reforms; revolution seemed too remote to contemplate.

It seems unlikely that anyone in the 1840's, even among the bolder spirits, except perhaps Bakunin and one or two members of the Petrashevsky circle, counted on the possibility of an immediate revolution in Russia. The revolutions that broke out in Italy, France, Prussia, and Austria had been made by more or less organised political parties, openly opposed to the existing régimes. These were composed of, or acted in coalition with, radical or socialist intellectuals, they were led by prominent democrats identified with recognised political and social doctrines and sects, and they found support among the liberal *bourgeoisie,* or from frustrated national movements at various stages of development and animated by different ideals. They tended also to draw a good deal of strength from disaffected workers and peasants. None of these elements was acticulate or organised in Russia in any sense resembling the situation in the west. Parallels between Russian and western European development are liable to be superficial and misleading, but if a comparison is to be drawn at all, the eighteenth century in Europe offers a closer analogy. The opposition of Russian liberals and radicals which, after the severe repressions following the Decembrist rising, had grown bolder and more articulate in the middle thirties and early forties, resembled the guerrilla warfare conducted by the encyclopædists in France or by the leaders of the German *Aufklärung* against the Church and absolute monarchy, far more than the mass organisations and popular movements in western Europe of the nineteenth century. The Russian liberals and radicals of the eighteen thirties and forties, whether they confined themselves to philosophical and æsthetic issues, like the circle gathered round Stankevich, or engaged in political and social problems, like Herzen and Ogaryov, remained isolated *illuminati,* a small and highly self-conscious intellectual élite; they met and argued and influenced each other in the drawing-rooms and salons of Moscow or St. Petersburg, but they had no popular support, no widely extended political or social framework either in the form of political parties or even in the kind of unorganised but widespread middle-class opposition, which had preceded the great French Revolution. The scattered Russian intellectuals of this period had no middle class to lean upon, nor could they look for help from the peasantry. "The people feel the need of potatoes, but none whatever of a constitution—that is desired only by educated townspeople who are quite powerless," wrote Belinsky to his friends in 1846.[1] And this was echoed ten years later by Chernyshevsky in a characteristic hyperbole: "There is no European country in which the vast majority of the people is not absolutely indifferent to rights which are the object of concern only to the liberals." While this was scarcely true of western Europe, then or earlier, it reflected the backward state of Russia. Until the economic development of the Russian Empire created industrial and labour problems, and with them tension between a middle class and a proletariat of the Western type, the democratic revolution remained a dream: and when such conditions finally materialised, as they did with increasing tempo in the last decades of the nineteenth century, the revolution did not lag far behind. The "Russian 1848" occurred in that country in 1905, by which time the middle class in the West was no longer revolutionary or even militantly reformist; and this time-lag of half a century was itself a powerful factor in causing the final cleavage between liberal and authoritarian socialism in 1917, and the divergence of paths between Russia and Europe which followed. Perhaps the late F. J. Dan was right in supposing that this was the parting of the ways which Herzen had in mind when, in his letter to Edgar Quinet, he declared, "You will go by way of the proletariat towards socialism; we by way of socialism to freedom."[2] The

[1] Quoted by F. Dan, *Proiskhozhdeniye Bolshevizma,* (New York: 1946) pp. 36–38.

[2] Dan, *Proiskhozhdeniye Bolshevizma,* quoting from *Kolokol,* No. 210.

difference in the degree of political maturity between Russia and the West at this period is vividly described in the introduction to *Letters from France and Italy* which Herzen composed in his Putney exile ten years later. His topic is the Revolution of 1848 in western Europe:

The Liberals, those political Protestants, became in their turn the most terrible Conservatives; behind the altered charters and constitutions they discover the spectre of Socialism and grow pale with terror; nor is this surprising for they have something to lose, something to be afraid of. But we [Russians] are not in that position at all. Our attitude to all public affairs is much simpler and more naive. The Liberals are afraid of losing their liberty—we have none; they are nervous of interference by governments in the industrial sphere—with us the government interferes with everything anyhow; they are afraid of losing their personal rights—we have yet to acquire them. The extreme contradictions of our still disordered existence, the lack of stability in all our legal and constitutional notions, makes possible on the one hand the most unlimited despotism, serfdom and military settlements, and on the other creates conditions in which such revolutionary steps as those of Peter I and Alexander II are less difficult. A man who lives in furnished rooms finds it far easier to move than one who has acquired a house of his own. Europe is sinking because it cannot rid itself of its cargo—that infinity of treasures accumulated in distant and perilous expeditions. In our case, all this is artificial ballast; out with it and overboard, and then full sail into the open sea! We are entering history full of strength and energy at precisely the moment when all political parties are becoming faded anachronisms, and everyone is pointing, some hopefully, others with despair, at the approaching thundercloud of economic revolution. And so we, too, when we look at our neighbours, begin to feel frightened of the coming storm, and, like them, think it best to say nothing about this peril. But you have no need to fear these terrors; calm yourselves, for on our estate there is a lightning conductor—communal ownership of the land.

In other words, the total absence of elementary rights and liberties, the seven dark years which followed in 1848, so far from inducing despair or apathy, brought home to more than one Russian thinker the sense of complete antithesis between his country and the relatively liberal institutions of Europe which, paradoxically enough, was made the basis for subsequent Russian optimism. From it sprang the strongest hope of a uniquely happy and glorious future, destined for Russia alone.

Herzen's analysis of the facts was quite correct. There was no Russian *bourgeoisie* to speak of: such middle class figures as the journalist Polevoy and the friend of Belinsky and Turgenev, the literary tea merchant, Botkin, and indeed Belinsky himself, were notable exceptions.

Social conditions for drastic liberal reforms, let alone revolution, did not exist. Yet this very fact, which was so bitterly lamented by liberals like Kavelin, Granovsky and even Belinsky, brought its own remarkable compensation. In Europe an international revolution had broken out and failed, and its failure created among idealistic democrats and socialists a bitter sense of disillusion and despair. In some cases it led to cynical detachment, or else a tendency to seek comfort either in apathetic resignation, or in religion, or in the ranks of political reaction; very much as the failure of the Revolution of 1905 in Russia produced the call to repentance and spiritual values of the *Vyekhi* group. In Russia, Katkov did become a conservative nationalist, Dostoevsky turned to orthodoxy, Botkin turned his back upon radicalism, Bakunin signed a disingenuous "confession" of guilt. But in general the very fact that Russia had suffered no revolution, and no corresponding degree of disenchantment, led to a development very different from that of western Europe. The important fact was that the passion for reform—the revolutionary fervour and the belief in the feasibility of change by means of public pressure, agitation, and, as some thought, conspiracy—did not weaken. On the contrary, it grew stronger. But the argument for a political revolution, when its failure in the West was so glaring, clearly became less convincing. The discontented and rebellious Russian intellectuals of the next thirty years turned their attention to the peculiarities of their own internal situation; and then, from ready made solutions imported from the West and capable only of being artificially grafted on to the recalcitrant growth provided by their own countrymen, to the creation of new doctrines and modes of action specifically adapted to the peculiar problems posed by Russia alone. They were prepared to learn from, and more than learn—to become the most devoted and assiduous disciples of—the most advanced thinkers of western Europe, but the teachings of Hegel and the German materialists, of Mill, Spencer and Comte, were henceforth to be transformed to fit specifically Russian needs. Bazarov, in Turgenev's *Fathers and Children*, for all his militant positivism and materialism and respect for the West, has far deeper roots in Russian soil—and that not without a certain self-conscious pride—than the men of the forties with their genuinely cosmopolitan ideals: than, e.g., the imaginary Rudin, or indeed one of the supposed originals of Rudin—Bakunin himself, for all his pan-Slavism and Germanophobia.

The measures taken by the Government to prevent the "revolutionary disease" from infecting the Russian Empire, did no doubt play a decisive part in preventing the possibility of actual revolutionary outbreaks: but among the important consequences of this "moral quarantine" was the weakening of the influence of western liberalism. The failures of the political revolutions, the feebleness and betrayals of the liberals, and added to this, the repressive acts of the political police directed against any symptom of subversive Western ideas, forced Russian intellectuals in upon themselves, made it more difficult than before to escape from the painful issues before them into a vague search for panaceas from abroad. There followed a sharp settling of internal moral and political accounts: as hope receded of marching in step with western liberalism, the Russian progressive movement tended to become increasingly uncompromising. The most crucial and striking fact is that there was no inner collapse on the part of the Russian progressives, and both revolutionary and reformist opinion, though it grew more nationalist, often took on a grimmer tone. It favoured self-consciously harsh, anti-æsthetic, exaggeratedly materialistic, crude, utilitarian forms, and continued to be self-confident and optimistic, inspired by the later writings of Belinsky rather than Herzen. There is not, even at the lowest point—during the "seven year long night" after 1848, that flatness and apathy, which is so noticeable in France and Germany during these years. But this was bought at the price of a deep schism within the intelligentsia. The new men, Chernyshevsky and the left-wing populists, are divided by a much wider gap from the liberals, whether of the West or of their own country, than any of their predecessors. 1849 was not a Russian funeral; it broke the spell of Western liberalism and faith in evolutionary reformism. In the years of repression, 1848–1856, lines of demarcation grew much more real; frontiers between the Slavophils and the Westerners, which had hitherto been easily crossed and recrossed, became dividing walls; the framework of friendship and mutual respect between the two camps—"the Janus with two faces but one heart"—which had made it possible for radicals like Belinsky and Herzen to argue furiously but in an atmosphere of deep regard, in some cases even of affection, with Ivan Kireyevsky or Katkov or Khomyakov or the Aksakov brothers, no longer existed. The quarrel between the moderates of the *Kolokol* and the St. Petersburg radicals in the sixties was genuinely bitter. Chernyshevsky's meeting with Herzen in London was a stiff, awkward and almost formal affair. Despite the continued existence of a common enemy—the Imperial police state—the old solidarity was fatally broken. The gulf between what became the left- and the right-wing oppositions grew steadily wider; and this despite the fact that the left wing regarded western ideals far more critically than before, and, like the right, looked for salvation to native institutions and a specifically Russian solution, losing faith in universal remedies compounded out of liberal or socialist doctrines imported from the West.

Thus it came about that, when at last direct western influence again reasserted itself in the form of the orthodox Marxism of the Russian social democrats of the nineties, the revolutionary intelligentsia which adopted it, had been brought up in a stern tradition not undermined by the collapse of liberal hopes in Europe in 1849–1851. Its beliefs and principles were preserved from contamination by the very hostility of the régime, and remained free from the danger, prevalent among their old allies in the West, of growing soft and blurred as a result of too much successful compromise, mingled with disillusion. Consequently, during the time of almost universal *malaise* among socialists, the Russian left-wing movement retained its ideals and its fighting spirit. It had broken with liberalism out of strength and not out of despair. It had created and nurtured its own tough-minded, radical, agrarian tradition, and it was an army ready to march. Some of the factors responsible for this trend—the independent development of Russian radicalism as it was born in the storms of 1848–1849—may be worth recalling.

Tsar Nicholas I remained all his life obsessed by the Decembrist rising. He saw himself as the ruler appointed by Providence to save his people from the horrors of atheism, liberalism and revolution; and being an absolute autocrat in fact as well as in name, he made it the first aim of his government to eliminate every form of political heterodoxy or opposition. Nevertheless, even the severest censorship, the sharpest political police, will tend to relax its attention to some degree after twenty years of relative quiet. In this case the long peace had been disturbed only by the Polish rebellion, with no signs of serious internal conspiracy anywhere, and no greater dangers to the régime than a few radical-minded university students, the brothers Kritsky, Sungurov, Herzen's friends, Belinsky's fervent readers, a few westernising professors and writers, with here and there, an odd defender of the Roman Church like Chaadayev, or an actual convert to Rome like the eccentric ex-professor of Greek, the Redemptorist Father Pecherin. As a result of this, in the middle forties the liberal journals, such as *Otechestvenniye Zapiski* or *Sovremennik,* took courage and began to print, not indeed articles in open opposition to the government—with the existing censorship and under the sharp eye of General Dubbelt of the political police, this was out of the question—but articles ostensibly concerned with conditions in western Europe or in the Ottoman Empire, and written in an apparently dispassionate manner; but containing for those who could read between the lines, vague hints and concealed allusions critical of the existing régime. The centre of attraction to all progressive spirits was, of course, Paris, the home of all that was most advanced and freedom-loving in the world, the home of socialists and utopians, of Leroux and Cabet, of George Sand and Proudhon—the centre of a revolutionary art and literature which in the course of time were bound to lead humanity towards freedom and happiness.

Saltykov-Shchedrin, who belonged to a typical liberal circle of the forties, says in a famous passage of his memoirs: [3]

> In Russia, everything seemed finished, sealed with five seals and consigned to the Post Office for delivery to an addressee whom it was beforehand decided not to find; in France, everything seemed to be beginning . . . our (French) sympathies became particularly intense towards 1848. With unconcealed excitement we watched all the *peripeteias* of the drama provided by the last years of Louis Philippe's reign. With passionate enthusiasm we read *The History of Ten Years,* by Louis Blanc . . . : Louis Philippe and Guizot, Duchatel and Thiers—these men were almost personal enemies, perhaps more dangerous than even L. V. Dubbelt.[4] Their successes depressed, their failures delighted us; contributors to our liberal journals might be writing about France, but the moral was quite clearly intended for their own country; they might discuss the campaign to liberate negro slaves—the analogy with Russian serfs was only too obvious, but difficult for the censors to admit, and therefore to punish.

Russian censorship had evidently not at this period reached its maximum severity; the censors were themselves at times inclined towards a timid kind of right-wing liberalism; in any case they were often no match for the infinite ingenuity and, above all, unending persistence of the "disloyal" historians and journalists, and inevitably they let through a certain quantity of "dangerous thought." Those zealous watchdogs of autocracy, the editors Bulgarin and Gretsch, who virtually acted as agents of the political police, in private reports to their employers often denounced such oversights. But the Minister of Education, Count Ouvarov, author of the celebrated patriotic triple watchword "orthodoxy, autocracy and the people"—who could scarcely be accused of undue liberal leanings—was nevertheless anxious not to acquire the reputation of a bigoted reactionary, and turned a blind eye to the less blatant manifestations of unorthodoxy. By western standards, the censorship was

[3] *Za Rubezhom,* Vol. 8, p. 123f.
[4] The effective head of the political police.

exceptionally efficient and severe; Belinsky's letters, for example, make quite plain the extent to which the censors managed to mutilate his articles; nevertheless, liberal journals contrived to survive in St. Petersburg, and that in itself, to those who remembered the years immediately following 1825 and knew the temper of the Emperor, was remarkable enough. The limits of freedom were, of course, exceedingly narrow; the most arresting Russian social document of this period, apart from the writings of the émigrés, was Belinsky's open letter to Gogol denouncing his book, *Selected Quotations from a Correspondence with Friends,* the full version of which remained unpublished in Russia until 1917. And no wonder, for it remains an exceptionally eloquent and savage onslaught on the régime, inveighing violently against the Church, the social system and the arbitrary authority of the Emperor and his officials, and accusing Gogol of traducing his calling as a writer, betraying the cause of liberty and civilisation and ignoring the character and the needs of his enslaved and helpless country. This celebrated philippic, written in 1847, was circulated in manuscript far beyond the confines of Moscow or St. Petersburg. Indeed, it was largely for reading this letter aloud at a private gathering of disaffected persons that Dostoevsky was condemned to death two years later. Four years earlier subversive French doctrines could be (so Annenkov tells us) openly discussed in the capital: the police official, Liprandi, found forbidden western texts openly displayed in the bookshops. The year 1847, when Herzen and Turgenev met Bakunin and other revolutionary Russian émigrés in Paris, and sent enthusiastic, if cautiously worded, letters home about their new moral and political experiences (some echo of which found its way into the radical Russian journals), marks the highest point of toleration on the part of the censorship. The Revolution of 1848 put an end to all this for some years to come.

The story is familiar and may be found in Schilder.[5] Upon receipt of the news of the abdication of Louis Philippe and the declaration of a Republic in France, the Emperor Nicholas, feeling that his worst forebodings about the instability of European régimes were about to be fulfilled, decided to take immediate action. According to Grimm's probably apocryphal account, as soon as he heard the disastrous news from Paris, he drove to the palace of his son, the future Tsar Alexander II, where an eve-of-Lent ball was in progress. Bursting into the ballroom, he stopped the dancers with an imperious gesture, cried loudly, "Gentle-

[5] N. K. Schilder, *Imperator Nikolai Pervy, Ego Zhizn i Tsarstvovaniye Primechaniya Prilozheniya ko vtoromu tomu.* (Notes and Supplements to Vol. II.)

men, saddle your horses, a Republic has been proclaimed in France!" and with a group of courtiers swept out of the room. Whether or not this dramatic episode ever occurred—it seems highly unlikely—the anecdote conveys the general atmosphere accurately enough. Prince Peter Volkonski at about this time told V. I. Panayev that the Tsar seemed bent on declaring a preventive war in Europe and was only stopped by lack of money. As it was, large reinforcements were sent to guard the "western Provinces," i.e. Poland. That unhappy country, broken not only by the savage repression of the Rebellion of 1831, but by the measures taken after the Galician peasant rising in 1846, did not stir. But Polish liberty was acclaimed, and Russian autocracy denounced as a matter of course at every liberal banquet in Paris and elsewhere; and, although this awoke no echo in Warsaw, then under the heel of Paskevich, the Tsar suspected treason everywhere. Indeed, one of the principal reasons why such importance was attached to the capture of Bakunin was the Tsar's belief that he was in close touch with Polish émigrés—which was true—and that they were plotting a new Polish mutiny in which Bakunin was involved—which was false; although Bakunin's extravagant public utterances may have lent some colour to such a supposition. Bakunin at the time of his imprisonment seems to have been entirely unaware of this obsession on the part of the Tsar and therefore ignorant throughout of what was expected of him. Hence he failed to include the non-existent Polish plot in his otherwise imaginative and highly accommodating confession. Soon after the outbreak in Berlin, the Tsar published a manifesto, in which he declared that the wave of mutiny and chaos had fortunately not reached the impregnable frontiers of the Russian Empire; that he would do everything in his power to stop the spreading of the political plague, and that he felt certain that all his loyal subjects would, at such a moment, rally to him in order to avert the danger to throne and Church. The Chancellor, Count Nesselrode, caused an inspired commentary on the Tsar's manifesto to appear in the *Journal de St. Petersbourg,* seeking to mitigate its bellicose tone. Whatever the effect on Europe, in Russia the commentary seems to have deceived no one: it was known that Nicholas had drafted the manifesto with his own hand, and had read it to Baron Korff with tears in his eyes. Korff too could scarcely keep back his own tears [6] and at once destroyed the draft which he had been commissioned to prepare, as unworthy. The heir-apparent Alexander, when he read it to a meeting of guards officers,

[6] Cp. Schilder, *Imperator Nikolai Pervy,* on which the account of this episode is based.

was in his turn overcome by emotion; Prince Orlov, the head of the gendarmerie, was unutterably moved. The document evidently stimulated a genuine surge of patriotic feeling, although it does not appear to have lasted long. The Tsar's policy corresponded to some degree of popular feeling, at any rate among the upper and official classes. In 1849, Russian armies, commanded by Paskevich, crushed the Revolution in Hungary; Russian influence played a major part in the suppression of the Revolution in the other provinces of the Austrian Empire and in Prussia; the power of Russia in Europe, and the terror and hatred which it inspired in the breast of every liberal and constitutionalist beyond its borders, reached their zenith. Russia was to the democrats of this period very much what the fascist powers were in our own time: the arch-enemy of freedom and enlightenment, the reservoir of darkness, cruelty and oppression, the land most frequently, most violently denounced by its own exiled sons, the sinister power, served by innumerable spies and informers, whose hidden hand was discovered in every political development unfavourable to the growth of national or individual liberty in Europe. This wave of liberal indignation confirmed Nicholas in his conviction that, by his example, no less than by his exertions, he had saved Europe from moral and political ruin: his duty had at all times been plain to him; he carried it out methodically and ruthlessly, unmoved by flattery or abuse.

The effect of the Revolution on internal affairs in Russia was immediate and powerful. All plans for agrarian reform, and in particular all proposals for the alleviation of the condition of the serfs both private and State-owned—not to speak of plans for their liberation—to which the Emperor had at one time given much sympathetic consideration, were abruptly dropped. For many years it had been a commonplace, and not in liberal circles alone, that agricultural slavery was an economic as well as a social evil. Count Kisselev, whom Nicholas trusted and had invited to be his "Agrarian Chief of Staff" held this view strongly, and even the landowners and the reactionary bureaucrats who did their best to put difficulties in the path of positive reform, had not for some years thought it profitable to question the evil of the system itself. Now, however, the lead given by Gogol in his unfortunate *Correspondence with Friends,* was followed in one or two government-approved school textbooks which went further than the most extreme Slavophils, and began to represent the institution of serfdom as divinely sanctioned and resting on the same unshakable foundation as other patriarchal Russian institutions—as sacred in its own way as the divine right of the Tsar himself. Projected reforms of local government were likewise discontinued. The "hydra of revolution" was threatening the Empire, and the menace of enemies within, as so often in the history of Russia, was given as the reason for further repression: such traitors were to be handled with exemplary severity. The first step taken was connected with censorship.

The steady stream of secret denunciation which issued from Bulgarin and Gretsch at last had its effect. Baron Korff and Prince Menshikov almost simultaneously it appears, compiled memoranda giving instances of the laxity of the censorship and the dangerous liberal tone to be found in the periodical press. The Emperor declared himself shocked and indignant that this had not been detected earlier. A committee under Menshikov was immediately set up with instructions to look into the activities of the censors and tighten up existing regulations. This committee summoned the editors of the *Sovremennik* and of *Otechestvenniye Zapiski* and reproved them strongly for "general unsoundness." The latter obediently changed its tone, and its editor-publisher Krayevsky produced in 1849 a *bien pensant* article denouncing western Europe and all its works, and offering the government sycophantic adulation at that time unknown even in Russia, and scarcely to be found even in Bulgarin's *Severnaya Pchela* (The Northern Bee). As for the *Sovremennik,* its most effective contributor Belinsky, whom nothing could corrupt or silence, had died early in 1848.[7] Herzen and Bakunin were in Paris, Granovsky was too mild and too unhappy to protest. Nekrasov was left in Russia almost alone to continue the fight. By displaying his astonishing agility and skill in dealing with officials, and by lying low for a good many months, Nekrasov managed to survive and even publish, and so formed the living link between the proscribed radicals of the forties and the new and more fanatical generation, tried and hardened by persecution, which carried on the struggle in the fifties and sixties. The Menshikov Committee was duly superseded by a secret committee (the Emperor was in the habit of submitting critical issues to secret committees, which often worked at cross-purposes in ignorance of each

[7] There is a legend still to be found in lives of the great critic that at the time of his death a warrant had gone out for his arrest, and it is true that Dubbelt later said that he regretted his death as "otherwise we should have let him rot inside a fortress," but M. Lemke (*Nikolaievskie Zhandarmy,* St. Petersburg, 1908) has conclusively shown that no such warrant had ever been signed and that the invitation to Belinsky to visit Dubbelt, which had largely inspired the story, was due mainly to a desire of the Third Department to get a specimen of his handwriting in order to compare it with that of a subversive anonymous letter circulating at the time.

other's existence) headed by Buturlin, and later by Annenkov—commonly known as the "Second of April Committee." Its duty was not that of pre-censorship (which continued to be performed by censors under the direction of the Ministry of Education) but the scrutiny of matter already published, with instructions to report any trace of "unsoundness" to the Emperor himself, who undertook to execute the necessary punitive measures. This committee was linked with the political police through the ubiquitous Dubbelt. It worked with blind and relentless zeal, ignoring all other departments and institutions, and at one point, in an excess of enthusiasm, actually denounced a satirical poem approved by the Tsar himself.[8] By going with a fine comb through every word published in the none too large periodical press, it succeeded in virtually stifling all forms of political and social criticism—indeed everything but the conventional expressions of unlimited loyalty to the autocracy and the orthodox Church. This proved too much even for Ouvaroff, and on the plea of ill-health, he resigned from the Ministry of Education. His successor was an obscure nobleman—Prince Shirinsky-Shikhmatov,[9] who had submitted a memorandum to the Tsar, pointing out that one of the mainsprings of disaffection was undoubtedly the freedom of philosophical speculation permitted in the Russian universities. The Emperor accepted this thesis and appointed him to his post with express instructions to reform university teaching by introducing stricter observance of the precepts of the orthodox faith, and in particular by the elimination of philosophical or other dangerous leanings. This mediæval mandate was carried out in the spirit and the letter and led to a "purge" of education which exceeded even the notorious "purification" of the University of Kazan ten years earlier by Magnitzky. 1848 to 1856 is the darkest hour in the night of Russian obscurantism in the nineteenth century. Even the craven and sycophantic Gretsch, torn by anxiety to please the authorities and, after Bulgarin, the most zealous of all the creatures of the political police—even Gretsch, whose letters from Paris in 1848 denounce the mildest liberal measures of the Second Republic with a degree of scorn hardly equalled by Benckendorff himself—even this poor creature in his autobiography [10] written in the fifties, complains with something approaching bitterness about the stupidities and iniquities of the new double censorship. Perhaps the most vivid

[8] Schilder, *Imperator Nikolai Pervy*.

[9] "Shikhmatov is Shakhmat (checkmate)—to all education" was a typical St. Petersburg pun.

[10] N. I. Gretsch, *Zapiski o moyei zhizni*.

description of this literary "White Terror" is the well-known passage in the memoirs of the populist writer Gleb Ouspensky.[11]

One could not move, one could not even dream; it was dangerous to give any sign of thought—of the fact that you were not afraid; on the contrary, you were required to show that you were scared, trembling even when there was no real ground for it—that is what those years have created in the Russian masses. Perpetual fear—that is the root of truth about life . . . panic was then in the air, and crushed the public consciousness and robbed it of all desire or capacity for thought . . . the atmosphere was full of terrors; 'You are lost,' cried heaven and earth, air and water, man and beast—and everything shuddered and fled from disaster into the first available rabbit hole.

Ouspensky's account is borne out by other evidence, perhaps most vividly by the behaviour of Chaadayev. In 1848, this remarkable man, no longer a "certified lunatic," was still living in Moscow. The *Teleskop* débâcle of 1835 had spread his fame. He seemed unbroken by his misfortune. His pride, his originality, and his independence, the charm and wit of his conversation, but above all his reputation as a martyr in the cause of intellectual liberty, attracted and fascinated even his political opponents. His salon was visited by both Russian and eminent foreign visitors, who testify that until the blow fell in 1848, he continued to express his pro-western sympathies with an uncompromising and (considering the political atmosphere) astonishing degree of freedom. The more extreme members of the Slavophil brotherhood, especially the poet Yazykov,[12] attacked him from time to time, and on one occasion virtually denounced him to the political police. But his prestige and popularity were still so great that the Third Department did not touch him, and he continued to receive a variety of distinguished personalities both Russian and foreign in his weekly salon. In 1847 he expressed himself strongly against Gogol's *Correspondence with Friends* and in a letter to A. I. Turgenev damned it as a symptom of megalomania on the part of that unhappy genius. Chaadayev was not a liberal, still less a revolutionary: he was, if anything, a romantic conservative, an admirer of the Roman Church and the western tradition, and an aristocratic opponent of the Slavophil obsession with eastern orthodoxy and Byzantium; he was a figure of the right, not the left, but he was an avowed and fearless opponent of arbitrary autocracy. He was admired above all

[11] Gleb Ouspensky, *Polnoye Sobraniye Sochineniy,* St. Petersburg, 1889, Vol. I, pp. 175–176; partly quoted by A. A. Kizevetter, *Istoricheskiye Ochezki,* Moscow, 1912.

[12] M. Lemke, *Nikolaievskiy Zhandarmy,* St. Petersburg, 1908, p. 451.

for his individualism, his unbreakable will, his incorruptible task, his integrity, and above all his proud refusal to bend to authority. In 1848, this paladin of western civilisation suddenly wrote to Khomyakov that Europe was in chaos, and in deep need of Russian help, and spoke with much enthusiasm of the Emperor's bold initiative in crushing the Hungarian Revolution. While this might have been put down to the horror of popular risings felt by many intellectuals—even so radical a thinker as Heine—at this time, this is not the end of the story. In 1853, Herzen published a book abroad containing a passionate encomium of Chaadayev.[13] As soon as he heard of it, Chaadayev wrote to the head of the political police, saying that he had learnt with annoyance and indignation that he had been praised by the notorious exile and followed this with sentiments of the most abject loyalty to the Tsar as an instrument of the divine will sent to restore order in the world. To his shocked nephew who asked *"Pourquoi cette bassesse gratuite?"* [14] he merely observed *"Mon cher, il faut tenir à sa peau."* [15] This act of apparently cynical self-abasement on the part of the proudest and most liberty-loving man in Russia of his time is tragic evidence of the effect of protracted repression upon those members of the older generation of aristocratic rebels who, by some miracle, had escaped Siberia or the gallows.

This was the atmosphere in which the famous Petrashevsky case was tried. Its main interest consists in the fact that it is the only serious conspiracy under the direct influence of western ideas to be found in Russia at that time. When Herzen heard the news, it was "like the olive branch, which the dove brought to Noah's Ark"—the first glimmering of hope after the flood.[16] A good deal has been written about this case by those involved in it—among them Dostoevsky, who was sent to Siberia for complicity in it. Dostoevsky, who in later years detested every form of radicalism and socialism (and indeed secularism in general) plainly tried to minimise his own part in it, and perpetrated a celebrated caricature of the revolutionary conspiracy of his day in *The Possessed*. Baron Korff, one of the committee of enquiry into the case, later said that the plot was not as serious or as widespread as had been alleged—that it was mainly "a conspiracy of ideas." In the light of later evidence, and in particular of the publication by the Soviet Government of two

[13] *Du Développement des Idées Révolutionnaires en Russie.*
[14] "Why this uncalled-for vile act?"
[15] "My dear, one must save one's own skin."
[16] A. I. Herzen, *Polnoye Sobraniye Sochineniy,* ed. Lemke, Vol. XIII, p. 591.

volumes of documents [17] this verdict may be doubted. There is, of course, a sense in which there was no formal conspiracy. All that had happened was that a certain number of disaffected young men gathered together at regular intervals in two or three houses and discussed the possibility of reform. It is also true that in spite of the devotion of Petrashevsky-Butashevich himself to the ideas of Fourier—he is said (not very reliably, it must be admitted) to have built a small Phalanstery on his estate for his peasants, who set fire to it almost immediately as an invention of the devil—these groups were not united by any clear body of principles accepted by them all. Mombelli went no further than the desire to create mutual aid institutions, not so much for the workers or peasants as for the bourgeois, like himself. Akhsharumov, Yevropeus, Pleshcheyev were Christian Socialists, A. P. Milioukov translated Lamennais. Balasoglo was a kindly and impressionable young man, oppressed by the horrors of the Russian social order—no more and no less than, for example, Gogol himself—who desired reform and improvement on mildly populist lines similar to the ideas of the more romantic Slavophils, and indeed not too unlike the nostalgia of such English writers as Cobbett, or William Morris. Indeed, Petrashevsky's encyclopædic dictionary which contained "subversive" articles disguised as scientific information, resembles nothing so much as Cobbett's famous grammar. Nevertheless, these groups differed from the casual gatherings of such radicals as Panayev, Korsh, Nekrasov, and even Belinsky. Some, at any rate, of the participants met for the specific purpose of considering concrete ideas of how to foment a rebellion against the existing régime.

These ideas may have been impracticable, and may have contained in them much that was fantastic drawn from the French Utopians and other "unscientific" sources, but their purpose was not the reform but the overthrow of the régime, and the establishment of a revolutionary government. Dostoevsky's descriptions in *A Writer's Diary* and elsewhere make it clear that Speshnev, for example, was by temperament and intention, a genuine revolutionary agitator, who believed in conspiracy at least as seriously as Bakunin (who disliked him) and attended these discussion groups with a practical purpose. The portrait of Stavrogin in *The Possessed,* largely modelled upon him, strongly stresses this aspect. Similarly, Durov and Grigoriev and one or two others certainly seem to have believed that the Revolution might break out at any moment; while they realised the impossibility of organising a mass

[17] *Dyelo Petrashevtsev,* Vol. I and II, 1940–1941. The third volume has yet to appear.

movement, they put their faith, like Weitling and the groups of German communist workers, and perhaps Blanqui too, at this period, in the organisation of small cells of trained revolutionaries, a professional Jacobin élite which could act efficiently and ruthlessly, and seize the leadership when the hour struck—when the oppressed masses would rise and crush the knock-kneed army of courtiers and bureaucrats who alone stood between the Russian people and its freedom. No doubt much of this was idle talk, since nothing remotely resembling a revolutionary situation existed in Russia at this time. Nevertheless, the intentions of these men were as concrete and as violent as those of Babeuf and his friends, and in the condition of a tightly controlled autocracy, they used the only possible means of practical conspiracy. Speshnev was virtually a Communist, influenced not merely by Dézamy but perhaps also by the early works of Marx—e.g., the anti-Proudhonist *Misère de la Philosophie*. Balasoglo states in his evidence [18] that one of the things which attracted him to Petrashevsky's discussion group was that, on the whole, it avoided liberal patter and aimless discussion, concerned itself with concrete issues and conducted statistical studies with a view to direct action. Dostoevsky's contemptuous references to the tendency of his fellow conspirators *poliberalnichat'*—to play at being liberal—looks mainly like an attempt to whitewash himself. In fact, the principal attraction of this circle for Dostoevsky probably consisted precisely in that which had also attracted Balasoglo—namely, that the atmosphere was not amiably liberal, gay, free, informal and intimate, and given to literary and intellectual gossip, like the lively evenings given by the Panayevs, Sollogub, or Herzen, at which he seems to have been snubbed and had suffered acutely. Petrashevsky was a remorselessly earnest man, and the groups, both his own and the subsidiary, even more secret, groups which sprang from it—as well as allied "circles," e.g. that to which Chernyshevsky belonged as a university student—meant business. The conspiracy was broken up in April 1849, and the Petrashevtsy were tried and sent into exile.

Between 1849 and the death of Nicholas I in the last months of the Crimean war, there is in Russia not a glimmering of public radical thought. Gogol died an unrepentant reactionary, but Turgenev, who ventured to praise him as a satirical genius in an obituary article, was promptly arrested for it. Bakunin was in prison, Herzen lived abroad, Belinsky was dead, Granovsky was silent, depressed, and developing Slavophil sympathies. The centenary of Moscow University in 1855

[18] *Dyelo Petrashevtsev,* vol. 2.

proved a dismal affair. The Slavophils themselves, although they rejected the liberal revolution and all its works, and continued a ceaseless campaign against western influences, felt the heavy hand of official repression; the Aksakov brothers, Khomyakov, Koshelev and Samarin, fell under official suspicion much as Ivan Kireyevsky had done in the previous decade. The secret police and the special committees considered all ideas to be dangerous as such, particularly that of a nationalism which took up the cause of the oppressed Slav nationalities of the Austrian Empire, and, by implication thereby placed itself in opposition to the dynastic principle and to multi-racial empires. The battle between the government and the various opposition parties was not an ideological war, like the long conflict fought out in the seventies and eighties between the Left and the Right, between liberals, early populists and socialists on one side, and such reactionary nationalists as, for instance, Strakhov, Dostoevsky, Maikov, and above all Katkov, and Leontiev and the Panslavists on the other. During 1848–56, the government, and the party (as it was called) of "official patriotism," appeared to be hostile to thought as such, and therefore made no attempt to obtain intellectual supporters; when volunteers offered themselves, they were accepted, somewhat disdainfully, made use of (Pogodin and Shevyrev were the most prominent), and occasionally rewarded. If Nicholas I made no conscious effort to fight ideas with ideas, it was because he disliked all thought and speculation as such; he distrusted his own bureaucracy so deeply, perhaps because he felt that it presupposed the minimum of intellectual activity required by any form of rational organisation.

"To those who lived through it, it seemed that this dark tunnel was destined to lead nowhere," wrote Herzen in the sixties. "Nevertheless, the effect of these years was by no means wholly negative." And this is acute and true. The Revolution of 1848 by its failure, by discrediting the revolutionary intelligentsia of Europe which had been put down so easily by the forces of law and order, was followed by a mood of profound disillusionment, by a distrust of the very idea of progress, of the possibility of the peaceful attainment of liberty and equality by means of persuasion or indeed any civilised means open to men of liberal convictions. Herzen, although he began to distrust and dislike Western liberalism before 1848, never wholly recovered from this experience. Bakunin was disoriented by it; the older generation of liberal intellectuals left in Moscow and St. Petersburg scattered, some to drift into the conservative camp, others to seek comfort in non-political fields. But the effect which the failure of 1848 had had on the stronger natures among the younger Russian radicals was to convince them firmly that no real accommodation with the Tsar's government was possible—with the result that during the Crimean War, a good many of the leading intellectuals were close to being defeatist; and this was by no means confined to the radicals and revolutionaries. Koshelev in his memoirs, published in Berlin in the eighties,[19] declares that he and his friends—nationalists and Slavophils—thought that a defeat would serve Russia's best interests, and dwells on public indifference to the outcome of the war—an admission far more shocking at the time of its publication, during the full tide of pan-Slav agitation, than the facts themselves can have been during the Crimean war. The Tsar's uncompromising line precipitated a moral crisis which finally divided the tough core of the opposition from the opportunists: it caused the former to turn in more narrowly upon themselves. This applied to both camps. Whether they were Slavophils and rejected the West like the Aksakovs and Samarin, or materialists, atheists and champions of western scientific ideas like Chernyshevsky, Dobrolyubov, and Pisarev, they became increasingly absorbed in the specific national and social problems of Russia and, in particular, in the problem of the peasant—his ignorance, his misery, the forms of his social life, their historical origins, their economic future. The liberals of the forties may have been stirred to genuine compassion or indignation by the plight of the peasantry: the institution of serfdom had long been an acute public problem and indeed a great and recognised evil. Yet, excited as they were by the latest social and philosophical ideas which reached them from the West, they felt no inclination to spend their time upon detailed and tedious researches into the actual condition of the peasantry, upon the multitude of unexplored social and economic data which had been so superficially described by Custine, or later, in greater detail by Haxthausen. Turgenev had done something to awaken interest in the day-to-day *byt* of the peasants by the realism of his *Sportsman's Sketches*. Grigorovich had moved both Belinsky and Dostoevsky by his tragic but, to a later taste, lifeless and overwrought descriptions of peasants in *The Village,* and *Anton Goremyka,* published before 1848. But these were ripples on the surface. During the period of enforced insulation after 1849, with Europe in the arms of reaction, and only Herzen's plaintive voice faintly audible from afar, those socially conscious Russian intellectuals who had survived the turmoil, directed their sharp and fearless analytical apparatus upon the actual conditions in which the vast majority of their countrymen were living. Russia,

[19] A. I. Koshelev, *Zapiski* (Berlin, 1884), pp. 80–83.

which a decade or two earlier was in considerable danger of becoming a permanent intellectual dependency of Berlin or of Paris, was forced by this insulation to develop a native social and political outlook of her own. A sharp change in tone is now noticeable; the harsh, materialistic and "nihilistic" criticism of the sixties and seventies is due not merely to the change in economic and social conditions, and the consequent emergence of a new class and a new tone in Russia as in Europe, but in at least equal measure to the prison walls within which Nicholas I had enclosed the lives of his thinking subjects. This led to a sharp break with the polite civilisation and the non-political interests of the past, to a general toughening of fibre and exacerbation of political and social differences. The gulf between the Right and the Left—between the disciples of Dostoevsky and Katkov and the followers of Chernyshevsky or Bakunin—equally typical radical intellectuals in 1848—had grown very wide and deep. In due course there emerged a vast and growing army of practical revolutionaries, conscious—too sharply conscious—of the specifically Russian character of their problems, seeking specifically Russian solutions. They were forced away from the general current of European development (with which, in any case, their history seemed to have so little in common) by the bankruptcy in Europe of the libertarian movement of 1848. Both those who believed in the unique Russian path (like Herzen and some among the Populists) and those who believed in objective social laws which ensured a similar development in Russia and the West (like the Liberals and Chernyshevsky) drew strength from the very harshness of the discipline which the failure in the West had indirectly imposed upon them. Henceforth the Russian radicals accepted the view that ideas and agitation wholly unsupported by material force were necessarily doomed to impotence; and they adopted this truth and abandoned sentimental liberalism without being forced to pay for their liberation with that bitter, personal disillusionment, and acute frustration which proved too much for so many idealistic radicals in the west. The Russian radicals learned this lesson by means of precept and example, indirectly as it were, without the destruction of their own inner resources. The experience obtained by both sides in the struggle during these dark years decisively determined the uncompromising character of the later revolutionary movement in Russia.

THE BACKGROUND OF THE RUSSIAN REVOLUTION *

E. H. Carr †

The Bolshevik revolution of October, 1917, did not come like a thunder-clap out of a clear sky. It had been preceded eight months earlier by the February revolution which overthrew the Czar and set up a liberal republican government. The February revolution was not only the product of two-and-a-half years of frustration and disorganization in the first world war; it was also an echo of the short-lived revolution of 1905 which had followed defeat in the Russo-Japanese War, and which now seemed in retrospect like a dress rehearsal for the major event of 12 years later.

The 1905 revolution had behind it a long trail of incipient or abortive revolutionary movements, beginning with the so-called "December" conspiracy of 1825—an officers' mutiny aiming at a palace revolution. The distant, faintly heard rumble of revolution had been the background of Russian history and, still more, of Russian literature and thought, all through the nineteenth century.

If, however, one seeks a convenient and arbitrary starting point for the story of 1917, the best landmark to take is the emancipation of the serfs by Czar Alexander II in 1861. The emancipation was an attempt to break up the feudal structure of Russian society, and to introduce into the primitive peasant economy the beginnings of industrial development on modern Western lines. In Marxist terminology, it was the first stage of the Russian bourgeois revolution—the same process set on foot in Western Europe by the French Revolution and its economic concomitant, the Industrial Revolution.

It was, like one previous important attempt to transform and modernize the basis of Russian life under Peter the Great, a revolution from

* The tide of revolution ran longer and deeper in Russia than it had in earlier revolutions in western and central Europe. It culminated in a revolution that was in many respects unique and can only be understood in light of the peculiarities of Russia's development, here sketched by E. H. Carr of Cambridge University.

† E. H. Carr, "The Background of Revolution," *Current History* (August, 1953), pp. 65–69. Reprinted by permission of Current History, Inc. For the early history of Marxism in Russia, *see* Leopold H. Haimson, *The Russian Marxists and the Origins of Bolshevism* (Cambridge, Mass.: 1955); on the impact of western values, T. H. von Laue, "Die Revolution von aussen als erste Phase der russischen Revolution 1917," *Jahrbücher für Geschichte Osteuropas* 4 (1956), pp. 138–158. *See also* W. E. Mosse, *Alexander II and the Modernization of Russia* (London: 1958).

above. The impulse came from within the ruling class, from a group of courtiers who had the ear of the Czar. Its motive was to remedy the chronic inefficiency and backwardness revealed by the Crimean War, and, by bringing the Russian administrative, military and economic machine up to date, to enable Russia once more to hold her own among the European powers.

But it was also a revolution from above designed, as Alexander II confessed, to forestall a revolution from below. In this respect it enjoyed a real, though equivocal, success. Short though it fell of meeting the needs and demands of the peasants, it went far enough to put an end to the long series of peasant revolts which had marked the course of Russian history.

But in so doing, it made certain that the Russian Revolution, when it came, would be infinitely more profound and more far-reaching. The emancipation and its consequences, direct and indirect, determined the course and character of the revolution of 1917.

By breaking the legal fetters which riveted the peasant to the land, the emancipation created the raw material of an industrial proletariat, and made possible the development of a "free" labor market. In other words, it played the same role in Russian history as the enclosures played in the early stages of the industrialization of Great Britain. The process developed slowly, and gathered momentum only in the 1890's, when the international conjunction of forces gave birth to a Franco-Russian alliance, and stimulated an abundant flow of French capital investment to Russia for the purpose of building up Russia's industrial and military strength.

Peculiar Development

Under these impulses Russian industry, and especially heavy industry, developed in the 20 years before 1914 at an astonishingly rapid rate. But the same impulses gave a peculiar twist to the industrialization of the Russian economy. First of all, large scale Russian industry almost from the moment of its birth was geared to the production of "war potential," including railway construction, rather than to the needs of a consumer market. It was "planned" in the sense that it depended primarily on government orders, not on spontaneous market demand; it was financed by loans accorded for political reasons rather than for the traditional "capitalist" motive of earning commercial profits. In these respects it anticipated much that was to happen in Russia under the Five Year Plans 30 years later.

Secondly, the tardy arrival of industrialization in Russia meant that it skipped over many of the earlier stages through which the much slower growth of industrialization had passed in Western Europe—the gradual transformation from the single-handed craftsman to the small workshop, and from the first primitive factory to the giant agglomeration employing hundreds and thousands of workers.

When modern Russian industry was born at the end of the nineteenth century, it immediately assumed the characteristic modern shape of the large-scale factory. Already before 1914, one quarter of all Russian industrial workers worked in factories employing more than one thousand persons each. In Germany the corresponding proportion was only 8 per cent; in Great Britain it was lower still. Russian industry, the youngest in Europe and in other respects the most backward, was the most advanced in respect of the concentration of production in large-scale units.

This hot-house development of Russian industry produced a social structure sharply differentiated from that of the older industrial communities of Western Europe, and falsified the prognostications of those Marxists who assumed that Russia would imitate, at a long interval of time, but without substantial modifications, the experience of the West and travel the Western democratic and capitalist road.

History, as commonly happens, failed to repeat itself. The rapidity and belatedness of Russian industrial development shaped the human factor on both sides of industry on distinctive lines of its own. In the West, something of the spirit of the earlier entrepeneur, attentive to the changing conditions of the market and in close personal contact with his workers, survived even in the manager of modern industry. In Russia, the industrial manager was from the first the administrator, the organizer, the bureaucrat. In the West, the industrial worker contrived to retain, even in the age of mass production, something of the personal skills and independent spirit of the artisans. In Russia, the vast majority of the new generation of industrial workers were still peasants in factory clothes.

A "grey mass" of peasants had been transformed overnight into a gray mass of factory workers. But to drive the peasant into the factories and force on him the rigors of factory routine required—before, as after, the revolution of 1917—a harsh and relentless discipline which shaped relations between industrial management and industrial worker on lines of a sharply defined class hostility. Weak and backward as it was, the Russian proletariat provided a far more fertile soil than the advanced proletariats of the West for the proletarian revolution.

The factories had, however, touched only the fringes of the Russian peasantry. When the revolution took place, more than 80 per cent of the population still lived on the land. The emancipation had freed the peasant from a legal status which had become an intolerable anachronism. But it had not solved the agrarian problem.

The peasant commune as a collective organ of cultivation was less, rather than more, efficient when the rights of the landowner had been abrogated; and the annuities now payable by the peasant proved not less onerous in practice than the obligation formerly owed by him to the landowner. What the emancipation did was to give the exceptionally capable, industrious or fortunate peasant the opportunity to rise out of the ruck and prosper at the expense of his less provident fellows, to acquire livestock and implements, to hire a worker or two, and set up as a petty landowner of his own—in a word, to become a *kulak*.

To encourage the *kulak* was the purpose of the Stolypin reform of 1908 in the system of land tenure, described by its author as a "wager on the strong." But, once again, too little was done and the time was too short. The prosperity of a few was enhanced at the expense of the increasing misery of many. The emancipation seemed to have staved off the revolution by lifting the burdens of serfdom from the shoulders of the peasant. But, in liberating him, it had destroyed the traditional structure of society and created no other. The peasant, cast adrift, could not make a revolution for himself. But he could, as the sequel showed, easily be harnessed to a revolution made by others.

Belated Reform

The political history of the Russian autocracy in the half century before 1914 reveals the same insecure and transitional character. Just as the emancipation of the serfs was a belated attempt to modernize the Russian economy on Western lines, so the political reforms which accompanied it were an attempt to bring an obsolete system of government up to date by borrowing and adapting Western liberal and democratic institutions. The courts were reformed, rudimentary social services were established, and an enlightened—though scarcely democratic—machinery of local self-government was grafted on to the rigid age-old trunk of autocratic power.

But, just as the Russian economy developed in a forcing house at a temperature maintained by pressures from without, so the political reforms grew not from the strength of their own indigenous roots, but under alien impulses from the West. They were accepted, reluctantly and with suspicion, by the rulers of Russia. Rarely has there been so striking a confirmation of Tocqueville's dictum that the foundations of revolution are laid when a ruling class loses confidence in its own right to rule.

It would be foolish to argue that Russia was inherently incapable of developing an industrial capitalist economy, or liberal democratic institutions, or of producing a commercially and democratically minded middle class and a thrifty and responsible "labor aristocracy" (to borrow Engel's convenient phrase). All these things had happened in the West. But, for history to repeat itself in Russia, it would have been necessary to isolate Russia from the external pressures of the West, so that events there could follow their own natural course of development.

What was not possible was to telescope into a period of 50 years the evolution of Russia from a primitive feudal society into a modern industrial democracy. Yet this is what was required if Russia was to catch up the time-lag and confront the Western Powers as their peer. Hence, in the ding dong battle waged throughout this period of Russian history between the traditionalists and the reformers (or revolutionaries), between those who thought that things were moving too fast for stability and those who thought they were not moving fast enough to catch up with the modern world, both sides were right.

Things were not moving nearly fast enough to put Russia on terms of material equality with the Western Powers. But the traditional supports of autocracy were being hacked away far too rapidly and ruthlessly for the halting efforts of those who were trying to raise pillars of society and government to replace them.

The story of the 50 years before 1914 explains why, when the revolution came, the whole edifice collapsed with a startling suddenness, leaving behind it a void of chaos and anarchy with hardly any constructive forces in sight. In 1905 defeat in the Japanese war almost gave the autocracy its *coup de grâce*. The proletariat of Petrograd revolted and tasted a brief moment of power in the first Petrograd Soviet. The liberals reiterated their demand for constitutional reform, and obtained promises which were not kept. The army hesitated, and stood firm.

A naval mutiny did not spread. Smoldering peasant discontents broke out, but too sporadically and too late to affect the issue. It was a trial of strength. But, once more, the concessions made, the reforms undertaken or promised, while they did not go far enough to allay the revolutionary ferment, went more than far enough to complete the discrediting of autocratic government. After 1905 the autocracy was a self-confessed failure.

When the storm broke in Petrograd in February, 1917, friend and foe alike were overwhelmed by the suddenness and completeness. The old order collapsed, not because new claimants for power were pushing it aside, but through its own inherent rottenness. No intermediate period of compromise with the decaying monarchy, such as occurred at the beginning of the French Revolution, was possible. Abdication was from the first the all but universal demand; attempts to secure continuity by substituting the brother or young son of the fallen Czar failed through lack of any broad basis of support.

Out of this void two potential governments emerged; the Provisional Government of the liberal intelligentsia, pledged to some form of constitutional government and using the watchwords of democracy, and the Petrograd Soviet, a revival of 1905, claiming to speak in the mystic name of "the revolution."

Dual Power

But neither of these forces was united or determined enough to govern a nation at war in the throes of an inextricable economic and military crisis. From February to October, 1917, in conditions of ever-increasing chaos, Russia lived under the so-called "dual power"—an uneasy compromise of mutual and grudging toleration between the Provisional Government and the regime of the Soviets (for these had sprung up, spontaneously and anarchically, all over Russia).

The Bolsheviks were at the outset a tiny minority in the Soviets. These were everywhere dominated by the peasant party of the Social Revolutionaries; in Petrograd and Moscow the Bolsheviks were, at first, outnumbered even by the Mensheviks. It was not till September that the Bolsheviks obtained a majority in the Petrograd and Moscow Soviets; almost everywhere else they remained in a minority till after the revolution.

Nor at the start were the Bolsheviks themselves united. Like everyone else, they had underestimated the breakneck spread of events in Russia, and assumed that the revolution there, having overthrown the Czar, would pass through its constitutional and capitalist phase. Only Trotsky, who had seen the revolution of 1905 at closer quarters than any of the other leaders, clearly realized that the basis for the intermediate stage, corresponding to the liberal democracy of the Western world, was lacking in Russia.

By the time Lenin returned from exile to Petrograd in April, 1917, he had come round independently to the same view, and forced it on his at first wavering colleagues. The record of events between the February and October revolutions of 1917 reveals that the Bolsheviks seized power, not because this was part of their original intention, and not because they had at first any large measure of support for such a policy. They seized power because the intermediate democratic regime which they, in common with all the other revolutionaries, had expected to see established, proved impotent.

This was the situation that Trotsky had foreseen, and which Lenin diagnosed from Switzerland in the first days after the February revolution. It is, of course, true that the Bolsheviks played their part in discrediting the Provisional Government and the parties in the Soviet which later joined the government coalition. But their power and their following were at first extremely small; and they could have made little headway against a government of even moderate strength and determination.

Like the February revolution, the October revolution was almost bloodless. In Petrograd there was no resistance worth the name. The Bolsheviks won because, once the Czar was overthrown, they were the only group who consistently showed confidence in their ability to seize and maintain power. Every middle road seemed to be blocked.

The dilemma which had opened the road to power for the Bolsheviks continued to beset the new regime when power had fallen into its hands. The feverish attempt to catch up the time-lag which separated the Russian economy from that of the West had proved fatal to the Russian autocracy. It had frustrated the ambitions of Russian liberals. The attempt had now to be made once more in the new conditions. No Marxist had hitherto believed that it was possible to make the transition, politically or economically, to socialism except in a community which had already passed through the stages of developed democracy and capitalism.

If Lenin and the early Bolsheviks now believed this possible, if they believed that backward Russia could catch up and surpass the rest of Europe, it was because they also believed that the proletarian revolution was imminent in Europe, and that the advanced worker could come to the aid of his more backward Russian colleagues.

When the hope of European revolution faded, the Bolshevik regime was faced once more with the old unsolved dilemma. How could the gap between autocracy and socialism be bridged in a country which had never had time to learn the lessons of bourgeois democracy? How could an advanced socialist order be built in a predominantly peasant country which had never possessed the resources in capital equipment and trained workers proper to a fully fledged capitalist economy? What would be the fate of the attempt of a socialist economy in Russia to catch up and overtake the economic development of the Western world

—an attempt which had already proved incompatible with the survival of Russian autocracy and with the hopes of Russian democracy? The answer to these questions was to provide the central theme of the history of the Soviet period.

THE BOLSHEVIKS AND THEIR RIVALS *

Leonard Schapiro †

History is seldom just to failure. The rapid rise of the Bolsheviks to power in Russia thirty-four years ago, their more surprising retention of power, the industrial and military achievements of the Soviet state—all these events have tended to create the belief that the Bolshevik dictatorship was the necessary and the only way for Russia. Now that opinion in the West has woken up, somewhat belatedly, to the nature of that dictatorship, it is interesting to turn back to the history of the early years of the Russian Revolution and to consider not so much those who succeeded, as those who failed. Were they merely rival aspirants to dictatorship, "supporters of a bankrupt order," swept from the field by the stronger team? Or did they try to guide the new Russia along a path which would avoid the horrors and inhumanity which are now found side by side with the material achievements?

The Russian autocracy collapsed in mid-March of 1917. Corrupt, distracted, and lacking support anywhere in the country, it crumbled in a few days. The fall of the monarchy had been brought about by no political party, let alone the Bolsheviks. The bread riots in Petrograd which led to its overthrow were the spontaneous expression of popular despair. The people were war-weary and hungry; the morale of the army after nearly three years' fighting was dangerously low. The maladministrations

* The Bolsheviks neither initiated the Russian Revolution, nor were they the only organized revolutionary group active in the upheaval. They constituted only one among several alternative groups and presented one among several alternative programs. In the essay that follows, Leonard Schapiro, Professor of Political Science, with Special Reference to Russian Studies, in the University of London, offers a glimpse of their rivals.

† Leonard Schapiro, "The Russian Revolution: Some Neglected Aspects," *History Today*, 1 (August, 1951), pp. 7–13. Reprinted with permission of the author and the editors. For a fuller treatment of the same subject see Leonard Schapiro, *The Origin of the Communist Autocracy* (Cambridge, Mass.: 1956). E. H. Carr, *The Bolshevik Revolution*, 1917–1923, 3 vols. (New York: 1951–53), is rather more tolerant of the Bolsheviks. *See also* Oliver H. Radkey, *The Agrarian Foes of Bolshevism* (New York: 1958).

of the monarchy and its advisers had contributed not a little to these results. Thus it happened that the fall of the autocracy was welcomed on all sides, but for different reasons: to the officers and to the upper and middle classes it meant an end of military mismanagement and new hope of military victory; to many millions of peasants in soldiers' uniforms it meant a speedy end to the war.

When, after centuries of autocratic government, a revolution unexpectedly releases a backward country from autocracy, it is obvious that unless that country can quickly create a moderate and yet authoritative government, it will lie at the mercy of any demagogue with resolution enough to seize power. A firm coalition between the liberal and socialist parties in Russia in March 1917 might have prevented the rise of Bolshevism by creating the necessary framework of order. Yet such a coalition proved, from the start, an impossibility. For this each of the parties concerned shares the blame, and the political history of Russia provides the explanation.

The autocracy had pursued a policy of suspicion and repression against all progressive elements in the country, drawing little distinction between the moderate reformers and the extremists. The constitutional concessions wrung from it in 1905 had been circumvented and frustrated. The result was that, in 1917, the three main republican parties—the liberals, the social democrats, and the socialist revolutionaries—were better versed in theory than in practice. Their experience was of conspiracy and interminable debate, rather than of patient and practical work in parliament, in committee and in trade unions. Now, in March 1917, with the sudden and largely unexpected removal of the shackles of autocracy, each party saw salvation only in terms of its own doctrine. With few exceptions, none saw it in terms of compromise, unity and determined practical effort. One such notable exception was the small independent group of social democrats led by Plekhanov, the founder of Marxism in Russia.

The liberals rallied without exception to the new republic, and formed the core of the Provisional Government. Their immediate determination was to lead the war to a victorious conclusion. Thereafter a Constituent Assembly elected by universal franchise would decide the future of Russia, and above all the burning question of the distribution of land to the peasantry. The position of the liberals was from the first unenviable. In the absence of a strong Russian middle class, their authority, indeed their survival, depended either on the backing of the army command, or on the backing of the socialist parties as spokesmen for the peasantry and the soldiers. But they failed to win this support from either side. The liberals first antagonized the army by yielding to the demands of the socialists and introducing a system of democracy in the army, which undermined discipline at a critical moment. They alienated it still further by refusing to take resolute steps against the Bolsheviks, who before long scarcely concealed their aim of seizing power. But they were not prepared, as liberals, to use the repressive methods of the overthrown autocracy against political opponents, however unscrupulous. They also feared that, if they called on the army for help against the Bolsheviks, they would be themselves overthrown by a military dictatorship. On the other hand, they antagonized the socialist parties primarily because such steps as they took to end the war in a "democratic" peace were not sufficiently radical to satisfy these parties. When the end came, the liberals found themselves abandoned by both sides—one of the factors which ensured the survival of the Bolsheviks in power.

The two socialist parties concerned were the Menshevik wing of the Social Democratic party (at that time a majority) and the agrarian Socialist Revolutionaries. The socialist parties did not at first enter into coalition in the Provisional Government. Their influence predominated in the Councils, or Soviets, which sprang up spontaneously all over the country, and particularly in the Petrograd Soviet. So far as the Mensheviks were concerned, as true Marxists they did not consider it their function to govern in the first phase of the revolution, the bourgeois democratic phase. During this period they saw their mission as one of control: their duty was to see to it that the liberal parties governed in the interests of the workers. They thus rapidly acquired influence without responsibility. The socialist revolutionaries, who claimed to speak for the vast peasantry, adopted a similar policy. Deadlock inevitably resulted. Repeated attempts were made to resolve this deadlock by uneasy coalitions, but their success depended on a spirit of practical compromise which neither of these doctrinaire and inexperienced parties possessed. At a time when nothing but drastic measures could have saved the situation, they were not prepared either to give the Provisional Government the authority to carry them through, or to seize power and carry them through themselves. They were not prepared to end the war by the simple expedient of walking out of it. But neither were most of them prepared to support the measures necessary for carrying on the war. They compromised by half-hearted support, coupled with loud demands for peace, which still further demoralized the army. They wanted immediate results from the revolution. But they were not prepared to help build the stable order on which such results depended, or to entrust the building of it to those who were perhaps alone capable of doing so.

The small Bolshevik wing of the social democrats, under the leadership of Lenin, who arrived in the capital from exile about a month after the revolution, adopted throughout a policy of radical and uncompromising opposition to the Provisional Government and to the other socialist parties. No serious steps were taken to restrict Bolshevik activities. In such conditions, the seizure of power by the Bolsheviks on the 7th November, 1917, presented little difficulty. The Bolsheviks promised the earth—peace, land, bread, freedom. In the major cities, at any rate, and in the army units which mattered, the ones closest to the capital, they rapidly won support away from the socialists. They did not when they seized power, or for that matter at any time since, enjoy a majority in the country. The elections to the Constituent Assembly were held a few weeks after the Bolshevik *coup d'état*. The Bolsheviks gained only one quarter of the votes in these elections, which a recent detailed study has described as ones in which "the vast majority of the electorate freely exercised the right of suffrage." The great majority of the Russian people voted for socialism, but not for Bolshevism. It was the fact that they were and remained a minority, and not the opposition of any extreme right or reactionary elements, which determined from the first the violent nature of Bolshevik rule.

While it was easy for the Bolsheviks to seize power, it seemed at the outset that they would have the greatest difficulty in retaining it. Yet the hesitation and disunity of their opponents assured them victory in the end. The attitude of the army was the first question upon which much turned. Though demoralized by weariness and by desertions, there were still more than sufficient units in the field to sweep the Bolsheviks from their insecure power, had prompt and decisive action been taken. No such immediate attempt was made. The troops, where they were not pro-Bolshevik, preferred a policy of neutrality to the possibility of civil war. The officers, in the first few critical days, were not prepared to come to the aid of the Provisional Government, which they distrusted little less than they detested the Bolsheviks. They may have hoped that, if the Bolsheviks got rid of the Provisional Government, they could then in turn sweep away the Bolsheviks. If so, they miscalculated their strength. Within a few months of the Bolshevik revolution, however, they succeeded in rallying a volunteer army in the interior of Russia to wage civil war. They were supported by a legion of Czechs, who in a clash with the Bolsheviks in May of 1918, fired the first shots. They also received some support from the Allied Powers, who were anxious to restore an Eastern front in the campaign with Germany. This front had been eliminated when Lenin proposed an armistice immediately after seizing power. The Allies now hoped that Russian armies would overthrow the Bolsheviks and carry on the war with Germany. For over two years, until the end of 1920, various anti-Bolshevik armies struggled against the new Bolshevik Red Army, and were all defeated. Their defeat was not entirely due to the valour of the Red Army, important as this factor was. Trotsky attributed the victory of the Bolsheviks mainly to the political ineptitude of the White Commanders. Their policy of restoring the land to the dispossessed landlords in the territories which they reconquered, and their methods of dictatorship, which yielded in no respect to those of the Bolsheviks, swung the balance of peasant support to the side of the Bolsheviks as the lesser of two evils. Trotsky, as the chief architect and organizer of the Red Army throughout the civil war, was in the best position to judge. The Allied intervention, at no time sufficient to turn the scales, also served to rally national feeling in the country against the invader.

The political opposition, following on the Bolshevik *coup d'état,* presents the more interesting problem. Lenin before long had to face certain difficulties inside his own party. Ostensibly power had been seized in the name of the All-Russian Congress of Soviets, a body upon which the Bolsheviks and their supporters had a bare majority, and in which the socialist parties were strongly represented. There had been nothing in Lenin's utterances to suggest that a one-party dictatorship was to be established, nor that the ordinary freedoms of speech and press were to be promptly suppressed. When forced, in November 1917, under the threat of a general strike by the union of railwaymen, to go through the motions of attempting to form a coalition with the socialist parties, Lenin astounded his followers by explaining to them in private conclave that he was merely playing for time. The simple railwaymen were in the end placated by a coalition with the dissident left wing of the socialist revolutionaries, whose views at the time were identical with those of the Bolsheviks. The impact of Lenin's duplicity on his party, together with the suppression of some socialist as well as of the liberal newspapers, led to a short-lived party crisis and to a number of resignations from the Bolshevik leadership. There was another minor crisis in January 1918 when Lenin decided to disperse the Constituent Assembly after one day's session. There was a major crisis in March 1918 when Lenin insisted on signing peace with Germany, on Germany's terms. He had repeatedly promised—before seizing power—that, if Germany refused the Bolshevik conditions of "democratic" peace, i.e. peace without annexations of territory of peoples, he would launch a revolutionary war. This revolutionary war, or popular rising against the imperialist invaders, was designed to kindle revolution in Germany and throughout Europe. With this promise now thrown to the winds, a serious revolt against Lenin spread through the Bolshevik party. Lenin weathered all these crises without difficulty. His personal authority over his party far outweighed that of any other leader. His opponents within the party understood only too well that their personal chances of survival, if they broke with him, were slight. Those who had resigned soon petitioned for reinstatement, and dissident groups acknowledged their error. Throughout the civil war the common peril cemented the Bolshevik party.

The liberals were immediately outlawed after the seizure of power and played little part in subsequent events. Some perished in prison, many escaped. A group of them survived in hiding long enough to help organize a plot for the forcible overthrow of the Bolsheviks. The plot was uncovered and many dozens paid with their lives. The socialists in the main repudiated the violent seizure of power, though groups on the extreme left of each of the two parties were willing to make common cause with the Bolsheviks. This collaboration was uneasy from the start and shortlived. As for the main body of the two big socialist parties, each adopted a very different policy.

The socialist revolutionaries, for all their antagonism to the Bolsheviks, hesitated to take up arms. At one time they hoped that the Constituent Assembly would restore them to their rightful position. Even when it became plain that this Assembly's existence was likely to be shortlived, they could not bring themselves to resort to force in its defence, though there were several regiments in the capital prepared to support them if they gave the order. Only when peace with Germany was signed by Russia did they decide to resort to arms, justifying the civil war as a continuation of the war against Germany, in whose interests they now believed the Bolsheviks to be acting. They joined the Czech legionaries and set up new provisional governments, on the Volga, in Siberia and elsewhere. Yet this resistance was brief. Before long the socialist governments had been swept away by more resolute White military dictatorships. Allied victory over Germany no longer made it possible to justify the civil war as a war primarily directed against Germany. The socialist revolutionaries were thus faced with the prospect of fighting Bolshevism under the banner of the White generals, and the great majority of them refused to do so. Some capitulated to the Bolsheviks; others escaped abroad to form an *emigré* party. Only individuals and individual groups continued the fight. It was such individual extremists also who were responsible for the risings, assassinations and the attempt on the life of Lenin in the summer and autumn of 1918, which were used to justify the official inauguration by the Bolsheviks of the so-called Red Terror in September 1918.

An entirely different policy was adopted by the Mensheviks. They chose from the outset to play the part of a legal opposition. Their aim was by political action in the Soviets and in the trade unions, and by written and spoken propaganda to turn the Bolsheviks from the method of dictatorship to a system of democracy, or at any rate democracy for all socialist parties. It was no easy task. Although officially outlawed for only a short period—from June to November 1918—they were confronted with a much more formidable campaign of illegal persecution. Their newspapers were suppressed, their activities interrupted by frequent arrests, and their chance of success in elections frustrated by every form of violence and chicanery. Yet, in spite of these difficulties, the Mensheviks achieved remarkable success. It is not possible to measure their success in election figures, since elections were rigged and were no indication of opinion. But by the end of 1920 the Mensheviks had the support of majorities in a number of important trade unions, and a wide following among the workers. What was more serious from the point of view of the Bolshevik leaders, their unceasing advocacy of democracy in trade union and soviet elections, of the elementary freedoms, and of some rudiments of legality in government, were beginning to find a responsive echo within the Bolshevik party itself.

The end of the civil war had brought a change in the temper of the Bolshevik rank and file. With victory achieved, they were growing resentful of the dictatorship of the Central Committee over the party. They resented the privileges of the party bureaucrats. They demanded the right to voice their criticism without fear of reprisals and to elect their own local party and trade union organizations without nomination from the centre. When, in March 1921, the sailors of the naval base of Kronstadt mutinied and demanded free elections, free speech, and an end to party dictatorship and administrative terror, they were supported by up to half the local Bolsheviks. Of the remainder, the majority remained neutral.

Faced with this situation, there were two alternatives open to Lenin. One was to yield to the demand for moderation and for some semblance of liberty. This would have revived some of the waning enthusiasm which the revolution had once evoked, and it would have allowed the development in Russia of the elements of order and self-reliance which the country had always lacked. But this course would have entailed the loss by the Bolsheviks of their monopoly of power, since they must inevitably have shared it at any rate with the Mensheviks. The other alternative, which Lenin adopted, was to launch Russia on the path which she has since pursued. The Mensheviks and the socialist revolutionaries still at large were eliminated from the political scene by arrests, which no longer, as hitherto, proved temporary. Opposition groups within the Bolshevik party were proscribed. Comparatively moderate men like Preobrazhensky and Krestinsky were removed from the party secretariat. A new party apparatus was set up, with Molotov in charge, soon to be succeeded by his patron, Stalin. Before long it became evident that the function of this party apparatus was to secure submission and implicit obedience to eliminate criticism and to ensure complete control by the Central Committee over all party activity throughout the country. Lenin had started the modern form of the one party state on its path. At the same time, by limited concessions to free enterprise he lulled the violent opposition of the peasantry to the Bolshevik policy of forcible food-requisitioning. These also made possible the revival of Russian industry, which had almost reached collapse. The Mensheviks had for some time been advocating just such a policy. It was not a coincidence that the initiation of it by Lenin was accompanied by their elimination from the political scene. In order to adopt their policy without admitting them to a share in the government, he muzzled them forever.

Lenin justified the eclipse of his socialist political opponents by an appeal to the argument of self-preservation. He argued that the Mensheviks and Socialist Revolutionaries were, wittingly or unwittingly, agents of the White Guards, of the imperialists, or of the secret services of foreign powers. This argument might appear more convincing if the elimination of Lenin's socialist opponents had taken place during the course of the civil war, when there was a serious threat that the Bolsheviks might yet be defeated. For the fact is that the socialist opposition was tolerated to some extent during the civil war, and only exterminated when the threat from the White Armies and from Allied intervention no longer existed. Lenin's argument has often been reiterated and is still to be met with. For example, Mr. E. H. Carr, after a short sketch of the socialist opposition between 1917 and 1921 in the recently published first volume of his *The Bolshevik Revolution,* concludes: "If it was true that the Bolshevik régime was not prepared after the first few months to tolerate an organized opposition, it was equally true that no opposition was prepared to remain within legal limits. The premise of dictatorship was common to both sides of the argument." This assertion is not altogether true even of the Socialist Revolutionaries. It is true only in that they resorted to arms against the Bolshevik régime after the Constituent Assembly, in which they had gained a majority, was dispersed by force; and that some individuals within the party were prepared to cooperate with the White Armies in order to bring about the displacement of the Bolshevik dictatorship by a military dictatorship. It is wholly untrue of the Mensheviks, the most important political opposition. If the history of the rise to power of the Bolsheviks is to be seen in the light of historical fact, then it is time that these ghosts of Lenin's propaganda were laid once and for all. Lenin's "legal" opponents failed because, although they had the moral authority, they were not prepared to use Lenin's methods in order to defeat him. Conversely, his opponents in the field, the White Armies, while fully prepared to use Lenin's own methods against him, failed because they lacked the moral authority to reinforce their arms.

It remains to consider why Lenin's opponents within the Bolshevik party accepted his new political policy. For no major Bolshevik leader was prepared to head those who opposed Lenin. It is significant that there was no open support for the Kronstadt mutineers within the Bolshevik party anywhere outside Kronstadt. Some of the Bolshevik leaders, such as Karl Radek, a future victim of Stalin's purges, saw that the weapon now being forged could some day be turned against themselves. Trotsky, who a few years later was to lead an opposition against Stalin on this very issue of inner party freedom, fully supported Lenin in 1921. There were two main reasons for this submission. In the first place, no one fully grasped the real nature of the apparatus of control which was being created. The knowledge that their own monopoly of power was in jeopardy, the panic induced by the grim reality of the Kronstadt mutiny, in progress while the party congress which passed the fateful new resolutions was in session—all contributed to obscure the issue. Some may have had apprehensions. But no one saw the simple truth that, if unlimited and uncontrolled power is put into the hands of one small group, the inevitable result must be loss of all freedom for all except the strongest and least scrupulous member of that group. But the main reason was the ascendancy which Lenin's personality had won over the party. The spirit which underlay the Bolshevik revolution was the spirit of surrender. The liberals and socialists had surrendered rather than face squarely the issues which confronted them. The Bolsheviks had, in turn, surrendered their will and judgment to Lenin when he led the *coup d'état* of November 1917. They surrendered again when the promises of freedom, of revolutionary war, of the workers' state, were successively shattered. It was too late for them to draw back now.

Thus Lenin's blind rejection of compromise and his bid for sole power both made the Bolshevik revolution and, in the course of time, destroyed what it stood for. According to Trotsky's accounts, Lenin died disappointed with what he had created. This may well be true, for there is some independent evidence of serious dissension in 1922 between Lenin and the new masters of Russia, Stalin and Zinoviev, eighteen months before Lenin's death, but after illness had removed him from active control of affairs. Few men in history can have made a greater mark on the fate of their country, and few men have thrown away a greater opportunity. In 1917, with his country reduced to chaos by irresolute leadership, Lenin had the courage to seize power into his own hands. One can criticize his methods, while allowing due praise to his resolution. But in 1921, when wisdom, vision, compromise, and moderation might have given Russia the beginnings of normal democratic development, he failed. His one lasting achievement remains that of having created an instrument of state tyranny, which in time completed the work he began—the elimination of moderation, tolerance, freedom, and responsibility from the political life of his country.

THE RUSSIAN REVOLUTION RUNS ITS COURSE *

Robert V. Daniels †

Inasmuch as the Communists have never been overthrown, some observers have been led to conclude that the Russian Revolution, reaching its peak in October 1917, has never left that point, and that Soviet totalitarianism is simply the revolution perpetuated in all its intensity. It can be shown quite easily, however, that beneath the surface continuity of the Soviet regime and its professed doctrine, fundamental

* One of the many merits of Professor Daniels's excellent work, *The Nature of Communism,* is that it distinguishes clearly between Communist revolution and Communist regime. Communist regimes, as is well known, do not all arise through revolution; nor do they remain revolutionary indefinitely. In the following excerpt from the above-mentioned volume, Professor Daniels (University of Vermont) shows that, as all revolutions eventually do, the Communist revolution in Russia ran its course.

† From *The Nature of Communism,* pp. 57–66, by Robert V. Daniels.

changes continued to take place. Developments which follow the pattern of revolution outlined above * can indeed be discerned in Soviet Russia. Overt and violent changes of government at each stage of the revolutionary process, while likely, are details which can vary from case to case and are not essential to the process itself. The basic emotional fluctuations of radicalism, conservatism, and authoritarianism, which constitute the essence of the revolutionary process, have made themselves powerfully felt in the changes which the Soviet regime has experienced in the course of its history.

When the Bolsheviks took power, the most extreme point in the Russian Revolution was yet to come. Initially the Bolsheviks coöperated with or tolerated the other socialist parties in the soviets, and moderated their plans for the socialistic reordering of the economy. Lenin called this the policy of "one foot in socialism." The most radical phase of the revolution began in the summer of 1918, when the Civil War broke out between the Soviet government and its opponents, the "Whites" (who ranged from moderate socialists through middle-class liberals to arch-reactionaries and proto-fascists). Terror commenced on both sides; fanaticism mounted; non-Communist political groups were outlawed in Soviet territory; violent "requisitioning" of the peasants' food stocks commenced; and an effort was launched to establish a completely socialized economy. This was the period of War Communism, lasting from 1918 to 1921, when the Whites were being overcome. So far, the parallel with the English Puritans and with the Jacobins in France is dramatically apparent.

In 1921, the Communists found themselves in a desperate state. Their utopianism and excesses were alienating more and more of the population, including many of the people who had originally supported the October Revolution. The nation was growing tired of revolution, while the chaos of civil war and class strife had brought the economy almost to a standstill. On the other hand, the most extreme and idealistic of the Communists were themselves becoming disaffected over the expediencies which the Soviet regime had adopted in its struggle to survive—especially its reliance on centralized bureaucratic authority and its failure to realize absolute equality of all citizens. The "Workers'

* *The Nature of Communism*, p. 51: ". . . the pattern against which we shall measure the Russian experience is this: accumulation of tension; breakdown of the old monarchical government; moderate revolution; extremist revolution; 'Thermidorian' reaction, preceded or followed by a military-like dictatorship; conservative trend, breakdown of the dictatorship, and restoration of the prerevolutionary regime; reaction against the restoration regime, and revival, in moderated form, of the revolutionary tradition."

Opposition," on the far left of the Communist Party, corresponded to the left-wing Hebertist faction among the Jacobins, or to the socialistic sects such as the Diggers and the Levellers in revolutionary England. The growing currents of opposition, both radical and conservative, combined to erupt in an armed challenge to the Soviet regime. Peasant guerrilla forces took to the field, and the naval base at Kronstadt (near Petrograd) revolted in the name of the October Revolution against the "commissar-ocracy."

Lenin's master stroke at this point, viewed in the perspective of revolutionary history, was to carry out his own "Thermidor." He proclaimed the New Economic Policy, and with it an end to the effort to reconstruct Russian society overnight. Primary attention was given to meeting the basic material needs of the population, even if this required broad concessions to the spirit of capitalism, and life for the average man began to return to normal. Revolutionary emotions were exhausted; relief was the general feeling, even among most Communists. The Republic of Virtue was at an end.

Such a shift to the right created the problem of disposing of the die-hard revolutionary extremists. They had to be curbed and purged, and Lenin set the wheels of his party machinery into motion to accomplish just this. The Workers' Opposition was denounced as a "petty-bourgeois anarchist deviation," condemned and broken up; it shared the fate of earlier idealist hold-outs, like Babeuf in France and Lilburne in England.

Suppression of critics on the left was particularly necessary for the Communist leadership if it was to continue to represent itself as the exclusively correct "proletarian" regime. Thus began the period when Marxism was fundamentally transformed, both in its meaning and in its use: it lost the power to guide, and was relegated to the role of justifying every governmental act after the fact, while for the rank and file it became a matter of obligatory faith. Viewed in the context of the revolutionary process, this change in the significance of doctrine was quite natural. If the revolutionary extremists were to hold power during the ebb tide of the next phase without repudiating their own creed, they would be compelled to resort to such casuistry, and to suppress the criticism which might expose their rationalizations. Engels once wrote of the revolutionary leader whose movement does not enjoy propitious circumstances, "He is compelled to represent not his party or his class, but the class for whom conditions are ripe for domination. In the interest of the movement itself, he is compelled to defend the interests of an alien class, and to feed his own class with phrases and promises."

The NEP was a period of bold pretension but cautious action. The Trotskyists, after they had fallen out with the rest of the Communist leadership in 1923 (when Lenin was already on his death bed), actually began to compare Soviet developments to the Thermidorean reaction in France after 1794. Such was the situation which prompted Lenin's successors in the party leadership—Zinoviev, Stalin, Bukharin—to begin the process of doctrinal reconstruction. Anxious or ambitious, these men would shield themselves with the cover of orthodoxy no matter where practical considerations might lead them.

It was only logical to proceed from the idea of Thermidor and look for a rising Bonaparte. Both factions actually began to do this; Trotsky's enemies could point out that as a popular military leader he represented such a threat, while the Left Opposition soon perceived the menace of Stalin. Zinoviev's partner Kamenev warned in 1925, after they had broken with Stalin and were at the point of joining Trotsky, "Comrade Stalin cannot fulfill the role of unifier of the Bolshevik staff. We are against the theory of one-man rule, we are against creating a 'Duce.' "

The Opposition's alarm was justified but futile. Stalin used his control of the party's organizational machinery to build an irresistible political machine, and then by adroit political maneuvering he eliminated all his rivals at the top level of the party. Simultaneously he put an end to the NEP and energetically launched his new policies of forced industrialization, collectivization of agriculture, and totalitarian control. The Thermidorean relaxation of the NEP had come to an end, as the new dictator applied the lash to evoke from the country an unprecedented effort toward the goal of industrial power.

The differences between Stalin and Bonaparte are obvious, but the analogy is nonetheless remarkable. Both imposed themselves on their respective nations at corresponding stages of the revolutionary process; both demanded and got the release of tremendous national energy. They differed, of course, in that France's violence was aimed outward in military expansion, while Russia's at this stage was directed inward. In the basis of their power the two dictatorships differed outwardly but were essentially akin: Bonaparte's prominence as a military leader and Stalin's success as boss of the party organization brought to power in both cases the man backed by the best organized group in the country. By the time of Stalin's triumph the Communist Party was permeated with military thinking and organization, and if it is viewed in its own terms as an army for waging class war, Stalin's regime can indeed be classed with the earlier cases of postrevolutionary military dictatorship.

From this point on the changes in the Soviet regime were much more subtle. The continuity of the leadership and its policies, at least until Stalin's death in 1953, makes it difficult to demonstrate any further stages in the revolutionary process. How could there have been anything, indeed, corresponding to the English and French restorations? A strong case can be made for the argument that Soviet Russia has never left the "Bonapartist" phase of dictatorship.

Rather than rest with such an exception, however, it would be preferable to revise our conception of the revolutionary pattern, to cover both the Russian and English-French cases as variants. What is common to both types in the last phases of the process? In no case was the Restoration complete except on the surface, while in the Soviet instance superficial continuity concealed an extensive shift toward prerevolutionary and antirevolutionary policies and ideas, both in the government and in the standards which it imposed on society at large. In every revolution at this stage there appears to be a strong tendency back to tradition, traditional values, and strong authority. Whether the postrevolutionary dictatorship is overthrown in the process is a matter of accident, and immaterial.

After the tumult of the First Five-Year Plan, the Soviet government under Stalin made its peace with tradition. In a series of steps taken between 1932 and 1936—i.e., after Stalin had consolidated his personal rule and had clamped tight party control on all spheres of social and intellectual life—the Communist regime turned its back on almost all of its heritage of revolutionary ideas and ideals. We have noted this trend already as it appeared in the development of Stalinist ideology. In one field after another, as practical problems arose, Stalin ordered the repudiation of the revolutionary norm and its replacement by conservative standards. Most observers, both sympathetic and critical, were thrown off the track by Stalin's insistence that the new line was correct Marxism, while earlier revolutionary ideas in practically every field were condemned as the reactionary outpourings of "bourgeois degenerates" and "counterrevolutionary wreckers." But such talk, as we have noted, was only the propaganda device whereby Stalin screened his maneuvers and sustained his self-righteousness.

We have seen at length how the Marxian theory of the state and its role in the historical process was turned upside down by Stalin, thus reversing the rectification of Hegel which Marx said he made. Soviet theory, like Soviet political practice, was brought into line with nineteenth-century conservatism, according to which the state, its continuity, and its leadership were decisive. In consonance with this shift the whole array of revolutionary expectations about the "withering away" of traditionally restrictive or disciplinary institutions—the state, law, school, family—was explained away or rejected outright.

Social relationships finally settled down in the thirties in a conservative mold. Social stratification rapidly became marked again. The government did not merely apologize for this, but welcomed it and actively encouraged it. Stalin asserted in 1934, "Every Leninist knows (that is, if he is a real Leninist) that equality in the sphere of requirements and individual life is a piece of reactionary petty-bourgeois absurdity worthy of a primitive sect of ascetics, but not of a socialist society organized on Marxian lines. . . . Equalization . . . , levelling the requirements and the individual lives of the members of society . . . , has nothing in common with Marxism, with Leninism."

Without much stretch of the imagination, the new ideas and policies of Stalinism can readily be viewed as aspects of a "restoration." Outworn revolutionary causes such as the persecution of the Church ceased to be pursued seriously; the final accommodation of Orthodox Church and Soviet State came during World War II. The virtues of patriotism and nationalist history were rediscovered, while the cultural autonomy of the non-Russian nationalities yielded before a stepped-up Russification. Modernism and revolutionary experiments in all the arts were suddenly assailed as works of the bourgeois devil; the field was left to the Victorian styles of "socialist realism." The bourgeois amenities returned—for those who could afford them. In place of the old class-warfare talk, legalistic and constitutional window dressing was set up on an elaborate scale, with the "Stalin Constitution" of 1936. The political priority of the working class for admission to the party and to higher education came to an end soon afterward.

While the "restoration" in Russia took place under Stalin's firm control, there was nevertheless a political upheaval to mark the transition: the Great Purge of 1936–38. The old anti-Stalin oppositionists, with Zinoviev and Bukharin heading the list, were tried and executed, but this was only the most publicized aspect of the purge. Simultaneously, most of the military hierarchy, the leading officials of the non-Russian republics of the USSR, and myriads of lesser functionaries were arrested on charges ranging from "wrecking" to treason. The number of people executed or sentenced to labor camps on trumped-up political charges in the "Yezhovshchina"—the campaign by Interior Commissar Yezhov before he himself was secretly disposed of—probably approached one million.

The climax of the purge came with the liquidation of almost the entire Stalinist party machine. The stalwarts who had come all the way with Stalin, excepting only a handful at the very top, were suddenly arrested, tortured, and executed. The operation was carried out late in 1937 and early in 1938 with the utmost secrecy, and the names of the victims, instead of being vilified like the Trotskyists, were simply cast into oblivion. As far as the rewritten history of the party was concerned, these men never existed.

The reasons for the purge of the Stalinists, as for the sweeping arrests among the officialdom at large, are still shrouded in mystery. Suggested explanations include such varied points as the need of a totalitarian government to keep its bureaucracy from feeling too secure, the secret police system running away with itself, and the personal paranoic madness of Stalin. For one reason or another, a deep cleavage had appeared between Stalin and the "Old Bolsheviks" around him. Historical perspective suggests (though direct evidence is lacking) that the split between Stalin and most of his prominent followers was connected with the basic change which occurred midway in Stalin's rule, from the earlier line affirming revolutionary goals though stressing the lengthy period and violent effort necessary to prepare for them, to an implicit contention that the goals were wrong all along. Stalin's oppressive, reactionary totalitarianism had reached the diametric opposite of the revolutionary dream.

Nonetheless, there were sources of strength in the Soviet "restoration," though unrest simmered and the labor camps swelled. The Second World War was a desperate test which Stalin's government passed, though it nearly went under in the first months of the German onslaught. Had this happened, the restoration would have proceeded from the change in substance to the change in form as well. But summoning the utmost in a disciplined patriotic effort, Stalin brought his country through the war far more successfully than anyone had anticipated; at the end Russia was stronger than ever. Only at this point, as war left power vacuums both to the west and to the east, did the export of revolution commence on a serious scale. But inasmuch as the revolution had run its course in its original Russian setting, its international extension proved to be more the reaching out of aggressive nationalism and suspicious *Realpolitik* than the proselyting urge of a militant faith.

If Soviet Russia has indeed followed the pattern of the earlier revolutions to the extent of arriving at a "restoration" in the nature of the political authority and in the substance of much of its policy, it would be logical to look further for developments corresponding to the last phase—the revival, in moderation, of the ideas of the revolution. Events since the death of Stalin in 1953 strongly suggest some such basic change, despite the limits in its scope. While the shift is once again beclouded by the continuity of the regime and its professed doctrine, there is reason to believe that Russia under Khrushchev has undergone a development analogous to the revolutions of 1688 in England and of 1830 and after in France.

In both France and England the significance of this last stage of revolution was to confirm the basic ideas and accomplishments of the revolution, to halt efforts to turn the clock back unnaturally, and to repudiate the excesses both of the revolution and of the restoration. Some of the revolutionary developments, such as the centralized and efficiently administered state in France, were of course never undone, and in Russia the state-owned planned economy and the Communist Party political monopoly clearly fall into this category. The significant changes in the final stage of revolution naturally bear on the most backward-looking aspects of the restoration regime. In Russia, these were the personal and capricious dictatorship of Stalin, his police terror, his xenophobia, and his conservative social and cultural norms.

Stalin's death brought the first of these aberrations to an end, and the reforms immediately instituted by his successors tempered the second. With the explicit attack on Stalinism made in 1956, the Soviet regime set its face at least formally against the most violent and autocratic aspects of Stalin's rule, although his record up to 1934—i.e., before the "restoration" trend and the purges—continued to be endorsed. The few surviving victims of the purge of Stalinists in the late thirties were amnestied, and the others posthumously rehabilitated. Most of Stalin's oldest and closest collaborators were dropped and condemned by the successor leadership—Beria in 1953, and the Molotov-Malenkov-Kaganovich group in 1957. Khrushchev claims to have dissolved the whole system of forced labor camps, and the Soviet citizen now enjoys reasonable security against arbitrary arrest.

In certain areas of doctrine and policy the Khrushchev regime has returned to older revolutionary norms. For the first time in three decades, it took steps to reduce economic inequality, by raising minimum wages and pensions, and gave increased attention to the main problem of mass consumption, the food supply. Particularly important was the reversal of the educational inequality encouraged by Stalin; tuition fees were once again abolished and the polytechnic ideal of combined mental and manual training was restored to favor. These steps were accompanied by a pronounced ideological shift, with emphasis on the role of the masses in history, and renewed stress on the future transition to the "communist" society.

In some respects the Soviet regime is not returning to the revolutionary spirit at all. For the most part, these are matters concerning the stability of society and the stability of international relations. The social stratification and bourgeois morality which are upheld in the USSR show no signs of losing governmental endorsement, while hypersensitive nationalism and the aggressive pursuit of national interest remain the rule in Soviet foreign relations. Both at home and abroad the Soviet regime is far more conservative than revolutionary. Domestic legality and international coexistence are professed as absolute virtues. All this still goes by the name of Leninism. The manipulation of doctrine to suit the convenience of political practice goes on as before.

Any effort to analyze Soviet Russia on the basis of a theory of revolution must, of course, be quite tentative. But as best we can tell from the sequence of policy changes and what we know of present social forces in the country, Soviet Russia has probably reached the end of its revolutionary journey. The political and social forms now established in the USSR are likely to prevail for decades. Communism in the dynamic phase of its revolution is now to be found only outside Russia.

DATE DUE

MAY 21 1970			
5-27-75			
APR 23 1980			